# Leading Adaptive Teams in Healthcare Organizations

Dec. 20, 2018

Wes,

It has been a real pleasure getting know and work with you. I greatly admire your work ethic and your dedication to furthering your own growth and learning – it is inspirational!

All My Best,

Kurt

# Leading Adaptive Teams in Healthcare Organizations

Kurt C. O'Brien and Christopher E. Johnson

3 Things to Think
About Regards Coaching

(1) Improve performance / Cut Better
(2) Train people + Self-comes
(3) Student self generates
       (self-development for
              Student)

BUSINESS EXPERT PRESS

*Leading Adaptive Teams in Healthcare Organizations*

First published in 2018 by
Business Expert Press, LLC
222 East 46th Street, New York, NY 10017
www.businessexpertpress.com

ISBN-13: 978-1-63157-172-5 (paperback)
ISBN-13: 978-1-63157-173-2 (e-book)

Business Expert Press Healthcare Management Collection

Collection ISSN: 2333-8601 (print)
Collection ISSN: 2333-861X (electronic)

Cover and interior design by Exeter Premedia Services Private Ltd., Chennai, India

First edition: 2018

10 9 8 7 6 5 4 3 2 1

Printed in the United States of America.

# Abstract

The objective of *Leading Adaptive Teams in Healthcare Organizations* is to provide specific frameworks, models, and skills that can guide healthcare leaders as they engage their teams in navigating an increasingly complex and uncertain environment. Topics such as creating a learning mindset, developing psychological safety, and creating a sense of ownership and mutual accountability are explored, and each chapter concludes with reflective questions for the reader to consider and potentially act on. The emphasis here is squarely on teams and the leader's role in leveraging collaborative group process to drive better patient outcomes. Because of the high level of complexity today's healthcare organizations operate in, we believe new frameworks and models are needed; this book is our attempt to contribute to this ongoing dialogue and body of knowledge.

# Keywords

adaptive, collaborative, healthcare, learning, mindset, ownership, teamwork

# Contents

# Acknowledgment

The authors would like to thank Carmen Mitchell, MPH, for her assistance with formatting and editing this work.

# CHAPTER 1

# The Importance of Teams

We would like to start with a story to help illustrate the importance of effective teamwork in health care, and how breakdowns in teamwork and communication impact patients and their families. This story relates the experience of one of our family members.

*My mom had been living with a painful shoulder for years, waiting for the orthopedic doctors to determine that her situation had deteriorated to the point that joint replacement surgery made sense—essentially when she reached the point where it became bone-on-bone. She was thrilled when she learned she finally qualified for the procedure, as she knew it would relieve the pain she had been dealing with so for long—not to mention that it would allow her to return to some of her favorite activities, such as gardening.*

*The procedure was scheduled for a Friday afternoon, and afternoon quickly turned into evening as the day's cases backed up. Eventually her name was called, and the surgery was performed. I was sitting with my dad when the pager went off close to 7 p.m. to let us know she was in recovery, and that the surgeon was ready to meet with us. He reported that all had gone as expected and that they had placed a block in the upper back/shoulder region to help with the pain, a standard practice with a good track record of success.*

*The next day she was feeling quite good, was pain free (due to the block), and the on-call physician assistant (PA) determined it was safe to discharge her. Of course she was excited—who wouldn't rather be home in their own environment? As she and my dad were getting ready to leave, she felt a few twinges of discomfort in her shoulder. The nurse assured her this was normal and that there was nothing to be concerned with. They gave her oral meds for pain control and sent her on her way.*

*My parents live on an island in the pacific northwest, so we decided it would be best for them to stay with us for a few days (just outside of Seattle) until she felt well enough for the trip north. They left the hospital and drove to the ferry dock (I live on a peninsula, a 30-minute ferry ride away). When* they arrived in the ferry line the pain had increased and she was quite uncomfortable. They called the number on her discharge papers and were told she should still go home and that she could take the oral meds. The pain continued to increase and soon her shoulder felt as though it were on fire. They decided it was time to return to the hospital.

They presented to the emergency department and chaos ensued. They had trouble controlling the pain, and the emergency department (ED) doc was concerned about infection—her shoulder was extremely discolored (we would later learn that this is actually quite normal with shoulder replacement surgery, but at the time it created additional concern and stress). There was no apparent communication or coordination with the orthopedic team, including the on-call PA, which led to ongoing confusion about her condition and how best to treat the pain.

Early Saturday morning she was finally admitted to an inpatient room, but there were continued challenges managing her pain, and confusion seemed to reign for the rest of the day. On Sunday I was able to make it over to the hospital and spoke with the charge nurse, expressing my concern with the lack of a plan and team coordination. She agreed and contacted the on-call PA (the same PA who had not taken the time to see her when she was readmitted to the ED), who finally, after more than 36 hours, came to my mom's room. The surgeon was eventually consulted via phone and a plan was established to manage her pain. Two days later she was finally able to go home to continue her recovery and rehab process.

Lessons learned from this experience:

- The orthopedic team had no contact or coordination with the ED physician after the readmission, a clear breakdown in communication that led to the ED physician raising concerns about infection, because she was unfamiliar with the procedure and didn't know that the trauma she saw to the shoulder and upper arm was actually quite normal. If the PA had connected with the ED physician, this confusion would have been eliminated.
- Miscommunication on the inpatient unit between the nurses and the orthopedic team—the nurse was concerned with my mom's condition, but was covering from another floor and was uncomfortable speaking up. I have to give the charge nurse credit for

*being assertive with the PA and calling attention to the situation and lack of a plan, but it took far too long for this to occur.*

- *The family members (or others who provide the support network for the patient) should absolutely be considered part of the team. We know this is controversial with some, but if I had not taken the initiative to voice our concerns (knowledge of the health care system was definitely an advantage) the delay in managing my mom's pain would have been even longer.*

Most people you speak with in health care today will tell you how important teamwork is to achieving effective and safe patient outcomes. The environment and processes are so complex that no one person can do the work alone. Yet many practitioners express dismay at how challenging it is to actually have good, effective teamwork. The folks at the hospital where Kurt's mom received her care were not bad people. In fact, once Monday rolled around, a team of nursing leaders swooped into her room to interview her in order to learn more about why the readmission had occurred (clearly, readmissions were something the hospital was closely monitoring, with the new pay-for-performance realities). They were thorough and certainly concerned about what had happened, and wanted to learn so they could correct the problems. The nurse manager was very receptive to the feedback and promised to convey our story/situation to other leaders on the floor, including physician leaders. The question still remained: how would they actually change practice to further minimize the chance that something like this would occur again? The answer is less clear.

Multiple studies have consistently demonstrated that clinical providers struggle with speaking up in instances where there is concern over a colleague's competence, clinical decisions that are deemed questionable from a safety perspective, being treated unfairly, being belittled, and so on. The Joint Commission estimates that upward of 70 percent of adverse events in health care are due to communication breakdowns and some safety officers we have spoken with believe this percentage could actually be higher (2005 National patient safety goals 2005).

One study conducted by VitalSmarts, entitled *Silence Kills* (Maxfield 2005), found that 90 percent of the time health care practitioners do not voice their concerns when dealing with issues such as competence, unsafe practices, and disrespectful behavior (to name but a few). This finding is simply alarming. Considering this from the patient's perspective, how frightening must it be to know that if one of our nurses, doctors, or techs saw something wrong that could potentially cause us harm, there is an extremely high probability they would say nothing.

In spite of this reality, the great majority of our health care organizations have not sat idly by, observing all of this from the sideline. Training resources have been devoted to providing communication skills, national and local conferences bring in expert speakers to talk about strategies for improving teamwork, and internal studies have been conducted in the attempt to discover key actions health care providers can take to enhance team functioning.

A variety of assessments exist that serve to provide feedback to teams about their relationships, communication skills, and performance—examples include the TeamSTEPPS Team Perceptions Questionnaire (TPQ) (King et al. 2008), Relational Coordination (Hoffer Gittell 2002), and Five Dysfunctions of a Team (Lencioni 2002). Many other home-grown varieties also exist. The challenge with these assessments lies in interpreting and taking action in meaningful ways.

We have been involved in providing organizational team training for many years, and have witnessed firsthand how challenging it is to truly create a culture based on teamwork. Good intentions abound, everyone wants to be able to work in effective teams, but these underlying difficulties persist, even in the face of overwhelming data and stories that call out the negative consequences of poor and ineffective teamwork.

So if it is not a case of lack of caring, then what prevents us from having more effective teams? We believe it has to do with a lack of knowledge, understanding, and appreciation of the complexities present in today's health care environment (Grol and Grimshaw 2003). We believe health care professionals need new models and frameworks that are more suited to the realities of today's environment, and that can result in new practices.

At the center of all of this reside the leaders. And we are talking about leaders at all levels of health care, from administrators and medical directors to the nurse and clinic managers. Theirs is a difficult job, seemingly becoming more challenging every day as the health care environment shifts, especially in the technology, regulatory, scientific, and political arenas.

To address this challenge our goal is to provide physician, nurse, administrative, and other health care leaders with ideas, strategies, and tools to create and lead teams that have a learning orientation, have the ability to self-correct, and get exceptional results. We need to get health care leaders thinking differently about teams, to understand how they can create an environment where teaming thrives, and how they must lead to generate creativity and exceptional results.

There are six specific topics we will address in this book:

1. Teams adopting a learning orientation
2. Creating a safe environment for practitioners to have a voice
3. The ability of teams to adapt and flex
4. Creating a sense of ownership within the team
5. Leader's role in team: dealing with specific group dynamics
6. Creating ongoing accountability

Each of these topics (Figure 1.1) will be explored in-depth, and we will offer strategies that leaders can apply in very deliberate and concrete ways, so that the teams everyone so desperately want can actually exist.

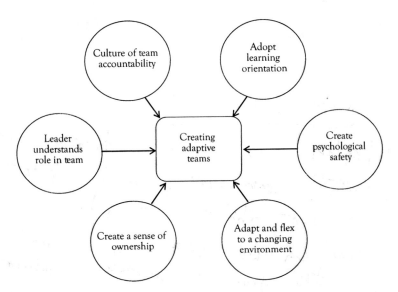

*Figure 1.1  A map for leading adaptive teams*

## End of Chapter Reflective Questions

- How would you describe the primary strengths of your team that contributes to excellent performance?
- What are the most pressing challenges facing your own team? What key factors are present?
- In what ways (and in what areas) does your team's performance fall short of your expectations? What factors do you contribute to this?

## References

2005 National Patient Safety Goals. 2005. Retrieved from www.jointcommission. org/PatientSafety/NationalPatientSafetyGoals/

Grol, R., and J. Grimshaw. 2003. "From Best Evidence to Best Practice: Effective Implementation of Change in Patients' Care." *The Lancet* 362, no. 9391, pp. 1225–30.

Hoffer Gittell, J. 2002. "Coordinating Mechanisms in Care Provider Groups: Relational Coordination as a Mediator and Input Uncertainty as a Moderator of Performance Effects." *Management Science* 48, no. 11, pp. 1408–26.

King, H.B., J. Battles, D.P. Baker, A. Alonso, E. Salas, J. Webster, L. Toomey, and M. Salisbury. 2008. TeamSTEPPS™: Team Strategies and Tools to Enhance Performance and Patient Safety.

Lencioni, P.M. 2002. *The Five Dysfunctions of a Team: A Leadership Fable*, 13. John Wiley & Sons.

Maxfield, D. 2005. *Silence Kills: The Seven Crucial Conversations for Healthcare.* VitalSmarts.

*Notes from hurt*

- *Leaders might have training in crucial conversations but staff are not skilled at it*
- *How can we create a team environment for the team to increase psychological safety?*

# CHAPTER 2

# The Learning Team

In 1990 Peter Senge published his best-selling book, *The Fifth Discipline*, where he ushered in a new wave of organizational thinking focused on creating a *learning organization*. He identified four elements that were necessary to create a learning organization: personal mastery, mental models, shared vision, and team learning. His point was to call out the need for organizations to adopt the mindset and practice of continuous learning, and how this particular mindset was essential for survival in an ever-increasingly complex environment (Senge 1990).

At the time, it became quite common to hear leaders declare that their organization was a learning organization, or that it needed to become a learning organization. For those listening to the message, it made good sense and we would all nod our heads in agreement, for truly this was the wave of the future. The problem was in how to actually make it happen. In fact, Senge himself fretted that the idea of the learning organization could simply become a passing fad, the concept du jour, as it were (Senge 1990). Interestingly, it was his ideas around systems thinking that eventually took on more prominence, likely because it was comprised of "archetypes" that were much more concrete, and thus seen as easier to implement.

Today, we continue to hear executive leaders in health care proclaim to large audiences: "We are a learning organization, and we are well-positioned to succeed in the future." While the idea of being a learning organization is still attractive, it has continued to remain abstract at best. How does one actually create a learning organization? Furthermore, what does it actually mean to *be* a learning organization?

In hindsight, this makes sense. The genius of Senge's work, from our perspective, is that he was calling out the complex nature of our environment and that a new metaphor was needed for our organizations, one that shifted us from the notion that organizations are machines, to

*Table 2.1 Comparison of learning organization approaches (Edmondson 2012; Senge 1990)*

| Senge | Edmondson |
|-------|-----------|
| Personal mastery | Teaming |
| Mental models | Organizing to learn |
| Shared vision | Execution as learning |
| Team learning | |

one that recognized organizations as biological entities that live, change shapes, and sometimes die. The field of complexity science (which itself was active during this time period, but little known) has consistently built on this over the past two decades, and is now generating more deliberate and actionable models (Decuyper, Dochy, and Van den Bossche 2010).

In 2013 Amy Edmondson published *Teaming: How Organizations Learn, Innovate, and Compete in the Knowledge Economy*, where she sought to make the idea of a learning organization less abstract and more practical. Her model focuses on creating a learning organization through the act of "teaming." Once teaming behaviors are well established, an organization must then structure and organize itself to learn. Lastly, the organization must then focus on execution as learning, which acknowledges the fact that the learning must be continuous and never cease (Edmondson 2012). Edmondson makes deliberate connections to complexity science and discusses how complex adaptive systems are able to self-organize and adapt in response to a rapidly changing environment. This is not possible without bringing an explicit and deliberate focus to the practice of learning. Our focus here is on the learning capability of teams. While we believe in the notion of the learning organization, it is much easier to conceptualize—and implement—a learning mindset at the individual and team level. (See Table 2.1 for a comparison of Edmondson's and Senge's perspectives on learning organizations.)

So what does it truly mean to learn? And more importantly, what does it mean to learn collectively? While Senge and Edmondson certainly offer useful frameworks, we would like to expand on their thinking by further exploring the following areas as they relate to teams creating a culture of learning:

- Mindset
- Adaptability
- Positive deviance (PD)

- Treating mistakes as learning opportunities
- Debriefing

## Mindset

Having a learning focus begins with establishing a mindset to learn. On the surface, this may sound like a relatively simple thing to do—or at least proclaim. After all, learning is something that has been a focus for us since we began our educational "careers" as preschoolers and kindergartners, eventually culminating (for many, but not all) with a college degree. This focus continues in many of our organizations where training and development programs provide opportunities for employees to gain new skills and abilities to make them more productive or efficient. In fact, one could say that the attainment of education is a goal espoused the world over, and many invest significant resources to help make this achievement possible ("Education | Global Partnership for Education").

Yet, when we look more deeply into our health care organizations we can find innovation lacking, and situations where staying with the tried and true becomes the norm—not because it necessarily works best, but because it is simply easier (Berwick 2003). Or worse, we have become complacent. It therefore becomes clear that education and learning are not necessarily synonymous. And what we need today in our health care organizations is more learning.

By having a learning culture, we are talking about a culture where exploration of new ideas is valued and considered the norm, where people are encouraged to speak up and collaborate, and where communicating openly across divisions, boundaries, and functions is a regular occurrence (Edmondson 2012).

Having such a mindset requires a fundamental belief that this type of learning is not just valuable, but is also critical to the future success of patient care and quality. Bruce Avolio, with the University of Washington's Foster School of Business, and executive director of the Center for Leadership and Strategic Thinking (CLST), believes leaders need to assess their "readiness and motivation to learn" and one way to do this is to understand our own preclusion toward having a learning goal orientation or performance goal orientation (See Table 2.2 for a comparison of learning goal and performance goal orientations.) (Avolio and Hannah 2008).

*Table 2.2 Comparison of performance goal and learning goal orientations*

| Performance goal orientation | Learning goal orientation |
| --- | --- |
| Focus is on completing tasks | Thrives on new challenges |
| May avoid risk | Failure equals learning opportunity |
| Feedback equals fixing something | Seeks feedback; feedback equals learning |

Leaders with a learning goal orientation are curious and frequently seek new ways of understanding the issues and situations that confront them. They want to move beyond existing practices, and have a true desire to understand the deeper workings behind the problems they are facing. In their book, *Managing the Unexpected*, Karl Wieck and Kathleen Sutcliffe call out the key traits of High Reliability Organizations (HROs) of preoccupation with failure, reluctance to simplify interpretations, sensitivity to operations, commitment to resilience, and deference to expertise (Weick and Sutcliffe 2011). Leaders of HROs engage others in this questioning to help get more hearts and minds involved in examining the issues at hand.

Leaders with a performance goal orientation are more concerned with meeting daily tasks and operational goals. The accomplishment of the project or task becomes paramount for them, and there may not be as much energy devoted to the learning process behind the task or project (Avolio and Hannah 2008; Dweck and Leggett 1988; Edmondson 2012).

While both orientations are needed (and beneficial) the leadership research clearly shows that leaders who adopt a learning goal orientation generally achieve better results (Avolio and Hannah 2008).

Yet another argument that supports the idea of having a learning mindset is Daniel Pink's enlightening book on motivation, *Drive*. Pink called out mastery as one of the three elements having the most significant impact on our intrinsic motivation. He describes mastery in very simple terms: "the desire to get better and better at something that matters" (Pink 2009). He discovered that an important factor in getting "better and better at something that matters" requires putting in the time to get better. In other words, practice and effort. Putting in this practice, and engaging in this effort, requires a mindset that the hard work will pay off in the end. In health care we must ask ourselves: how do we make it possible for our teams to gain mastery?

To get better at what matters most to us, which is providing the highest quality and safest care in a way that respectfully engages the patient, we must not just support our teams, but we must take it to a higher level by engendering a learning mindset, one that gives them control over diagnosing and solving problems, and encourages their continual development in an effort of working toward mastery.

Questions to help you understand if you are engendering a learning mindset:

- Do you regularly ask your team members for their ideas on how to address problems (either recurring or acute)?
- When team members come to you, as the leader, and ask you to solve their problem, how do you respond? Do you take on their problem as your own, or do you ask them questions and encourage them to keep at it?
- To what extent do you question your own biases and assumptions? (also see Chapter 4)

## Adaptability

We all recognize that our environment is constantly changing and the days of finding stability in our work places are largely a thing of the past. In the 1980s Shell Oil tackled this reality by revolutionizing the practice of scenario planning (De Geus 2002; Schwartz 1996). Its objective was to collect as much information as possible about the environment, and it used many different sources for this, looking well beyond the energy and petroleum sectors (e.g., political, social, technological, and so on). With the information in hand, teams would create various scenarios that could potentially come true. Eventually they would settle on three to five scenarios and would then ask: "How will we respond if this potential future happens?" It proved to be a powerful way to anticipate change and allowed them ultimately to be more adaptive and flexible as the environment continued to shift.

Consider our current health care environment for a moment: we are seeing unprecedented levels of change (e.g., accountable care, pay for performance, meaningful use, big data, health care grades, telemedicine, and other technological innovations). In speaking with leaders at all levels one consistent theme we continue to hear is the challenge and difficulty leaders are having in responding to these massive and continuous changes. Leaders report feeling overwhelmed, stressed, anxious, and worried that they may have missed something because they can't possibly keep up with everything coming at them.

We assert that our response should be one of getting more comfortable being uncomfortable. We need to become more adaptive, more flexible. While this is a simple statement, and it sounds like the right thing to do, it really is more of an abstraction—"Sure, I'll just come in tomorrow and I will be more adaptive!" Yet there are in fact some concrete skills we can employ to assist us with becoming more adaptive.

- Conduct regular environmental scans, and include your entire team (see Chapter 4 for more detailed information on conducting an environmental scan)—regularly engaging the team in the process of scanning the environment helps the team create a shared mental model of not only what they are seeing, but how they actually experience the environment around them. Since we all view the world through different lenses, giving the team the chance to periodically get explicit about what they are viewing helps reduce the instances of working at cross-purposes, and also provides clarity about new goals and improvement opportunities.
- Further develop the emotional intelligence competency, *flexibility*—at an individual level; flexibility involves stepping back from a situation and viewing it with fresh eyes, acknowledging that we may not hold all of the answers and that we need to turn to others (or other resources) to see the situation more clearly. At the team level, individual members can feed off of each other by openly exploring different approaches, or asking questions to better understand why something may not be working the way they thought it would (the question

listed in the next bullet is yet another way to encourage more flexibility).

- Deliberately ask the question, "If this were to happen, what would be the impact on us? How would we respond?" Leading the team through this mental exercise, which takes a page from the process of scenario planning, helps reduce the potential for "group think," and also forces members of the team to get outside of their own heads, as it were. By role modeling this behavior, the leader can set the expectation of always thinking beyond the current situation—literally expanding the thinking capacity of the team.

## Positive Deviance

Finding what is already working really well, despite challenges, learning about it, and figuring out how to replicate it, is the essence of PD. The reality in our health care organizations is that our teams are conditioned to focus on problems and what is not working. We are also constantly confronting what is known as the "normalization of deviance." This condition arises when we get so comfortable with the current processes and ways of doing our work that we get complacent in continuing to pay attention to important details. Consider the example of learning to drive a car for the first time. Think back to that moment and reflect on the actions you took when you climbed behind the wheel—seat adjusted, seat belt fastened, mirrors adjusted, radio off (to limit distractions)—the list goes on. Now consider the actions you took when getting in your car to get to work, or the grocery store, or the kids soccer game—latte in hand, iPod plugged in, checking text messages—clearly, it is a different level of preparation and our safety is compromised; yet we continue to engage in this unsafe behavior day in and day out.

Examples of PD with health care teams certainly exist in our organizations—we just need to do a better job of seeking them out and learning from them. So this relates back to having a learning mindset. A wonderful example of applying PD is provided by Jerry Sternin, who traveled to Vietnam in 1990 to assist the government with addressing its child malnutrition. At that time, 65 percent of children under the age of three were malnourished. Sternin and his small team visited four villages and discovered that, even among these very poor families, a small number of children were actually not malnourished, and were in fact quite healthy.

He discovered that the parents of these children practiced a different habit of feeding their children. Rather than feeding their children twice a day (as was the normal practice in most households) these parents fed their children four to five times a day with smaller portions. Additionally, they added protein, in the form of shrimp and crab, and also added small amounts of sweet potato greens. His team, working with the various members of the villages, had discovered a reliable solution to the problem. They continued to work with the villagers to develop a process for helping other parents create this habit, and after several weeks 40 percent of children who had participated in this test were no longer malnourished, and an additional 20 percent had transitioned from being severely malnourished to moderately malnourished (Heath and Heath 2010; Marsh, Schroeder, Dearden, Sternin, and Sternin 2004).

Keith McCandless and Henri Lipmanowicz, and their work with Liberating Structures, make use of the concept of PD with their microstructure appreciative interviewing (Liberating Structures 2016). For example, in an effort to reduce hospital-acquired infections, Dr. Michael Gardam and his research team interviewed health care providers and teams to elicit successful examples of how they were working to prevent infections. After collecting these stories, they were able to share the practices with other providers, reinforcing the ability of frontline staff to make a difference in care (Liberating Structures 2016).

Therefore, leaders should seriously consider routinely identifying other teams in their organization (or outside the organization, if appropriate) that are getting outstanding results, are finding innovative solutions, and have adopted a learning mentality.

## Treat Mistakes as Learning Opportunities

If we are to create a culture of learning, we must overcome our habit of punishing mistakes. Our society thrives on focusing on problems, identifying what went wrong, and then handing out blame. This is certainly the case in our political circles, our communities, and our health care organizations. These practices do not aid in creating a learning environment, and in fact actually work against it.

Amy Edmondson identifies a key leader behavior as framing situations as learning opportunities (Edmondson 2012). If our natural default state is to critique, criticize, or blame when a mistake occurs, the result will likely be one of self-preservation by the parties involved. Leaders, therefore, need to take the deliberate step of telling their teams that while the goal may still be to be error free, when errors or mistakes do occur, they will seek to understand the cause of the mistake so that appropriate changes can be made in order to prevent the same mistake from occurring in the future (Note: in cases where protocols or policies were deliberately ignored, or where specific intent existed to cause an error or harm, this approach does not apply, and the organization should take action to address the behavior).

Bringing the team together after an event, and openly exploring the reasons behind the mistake, creates shared ownership by the entire team. Once this level of diagnosis has occurred, the team can begin to look for ways to address the mistake, whether that be making changes to existing practices or policies, or developing new, innovative approaches to deal with the problem at hand.

## Debrief

Related to the previous issue of getting comfortable with making mistakes, there is one practice we would like to call out as being particularly effective in creating a learning culture—the debrief.

The U.S. Army regularly conducts *after action reviews* (AARs) after operations; while leaders generally initiate these, the entire team participates and everyone is expected to offer their observations, the sole purpose being that they can learn what worked and didn't work so they can make changes in the future.

While working with a group of surgical residents on identifying and practicing certain emotional intelligence skills, one of their attending physicians related a story from his days as a resident. During a surgical procedure, his attending physician instructed him to clamp and cut a duct. Believing he was getting ready to cut the ureter, he brought this to the attending physician's attention. The response he received was pointed: "Cut it, and do it now!" Of course it did in fact turn out to be the ureter, which now had to be repaired. He took the appropriate action of speaking up, but the attending physician's single-minded focus resulted in a preventable medical error.

Mistakes like these, unfortunately, still occur far too often in medicine. From our standpoint, the issue isn't so much about the mistake (which certainly should not have occurred), but rather with the process. After this event, a debrief (or AAR) was never held, so there was no opportunity for the surgical team to turn the event into a learning opportunity, hopefully preventing the same mistake from ever happening again.

The team training program TeamSTEPPS advocates for the regular practice of debriefing. Leaders play a critical role by modeling the debrief where three questions are asked of the team:

1. What went well?
2. What didn't go as planned?
3. What can we do differently next time?

It is critical to always begin by addressing what worked well. Health care providers are so accustomed to focusing on what is not working (with the good intentions of fixing things and making improvements) that they often forget to identify and call out what they are doing well. Then the team can move on to discussing the other two questions and identifying what they can do better next time. This is really about creating a habit, being extremely rigorous conducting debriefs (also referred to as reflection, AARs); if this process is not hardwired by teams, continuous learning is not possible.

## Summary

If our health care teams are to become more effective in this ever-changing, complex environment, adopting a learning orientation can be a key strategy. Focusing on the areas of creating a learning mindset, being deliberately adaptive, researching the positive outcomes of other teams (PD), treating mistakes as learning opportunities, and conducting regular debriefs to learn what has worked and hasn't worked could be useful to teams striving to take their performance to the next level. Shifting from a focus of problem solving to one of learning can help teams respond more productively to a changing environment, while also providing more support and satisfaction for team members.

## End of Chapter Reflective Questions

- Assess your own orientation to learning—how would you describe your own learning mindset? What more could you do to foster a learning environment within your team?
- How can you deliberately seek out examples of efforts in your organization, or within your team, that are working well? How can you learn from their example?
- How do you handle mistakes when they occur? What is an example of a recent mistake that has occurred with your team? How did you handle it? How could you frame it as a learning opportunity?

## References

Avolio, B.J., and S.T. Hannah. 2008. "Developmental Readiness: Accelerating Leader Development." *Consulting Psychology Journal: Practice and Research* 60, no. 4, p. 331.

Berwick, D.M. 2003. "Disseminating Innovations in Health Care." *Jama* 289, no. 15, pp. 1969–75.

De Geus, A. 2002. *The Living Company: Habits for Survival in a Turbulent Business.* Boston, MA: Harvard Business Review Press.

Decuyper, S., F. Dochy, and P. Van den Bossche. 2010. "Grasping the Dynamic Complexity of Team Learning: An Integrative Model for Effective Team Learning in Organisations." *Educational Research Review* 5, no. 2, pp. 111–33.

Dweck, C.S., and E.L. Leggett. 1988. "A Social-Cognitive Approach to Motivation and Personality." *Psychological review* 95, no. 2, p. 256.

Edmondson, A.C. 2012. *Teaming: How Organizations Learn, Innovate, and Compete in the Knowledge Economy.* John Wiley & Sons.

Education | Global Partnership for Education. Retrieved from http://globalpartnership.org/education

Heath, C., and D. Heath. 2010. *Switch: How to Change When Change is Hard.* New York: Broadway Books.

Liberating Structures 2016. Retrieved from http://liberatingstructures.com/

Marsh, D.R., D.G. Schroeder, K.A. Dearden, J. Sternin, and M. Sternin. 2004. "The Power of Positive Deviance." *BMJ: British Medical Journal* 329, no. 7475, p. 1177.

Pink, D.H. 2009. *Drive: The Surprising Truth about What Motivates Us, 138*, 240. New York: Penguin Group, Inc.

Schwartz, P. 1996. *The Art of the Long View: Paths to Strategic Insight for Yourself and Your Company*. Crown Business.

Senge, P. 1990. *The Fifth Discipline: The Art and Science of the Learning Organization*. New York: Currency Doubleday.

Weick, K.E., and K.M. Sutcliffe. 2011. *Managing the Unexpected: Resilient Performance in an Age of Uncertainty, 8*. John Wiley & Sons.

# CHAPTER 3

# Making It Safe to Team

In order for teams to work effectively and to have a culture of learning, there are specific skills that need to be employed—and leaders play a significant role in making it possible for these skills to be implemented. At the core is the ability to create the conditions of psychological safety so team members feel free and safe to speak up.

Creating these conditions is dependent on practicing certain skills such as balancing advocacy with inquiry to emphasize curiosity and listening and not just advocating for one's own point of view. It also entails practicing empathy so that others' needs are fully understood and appreciated, which aids in more rapid resolution of conflict when it arises.

Significant emphasis is currently being placed on this concept of psychological safety (or making it safe to speak up) in health care, and there is ample evidence of the consequences when we fail to speak up. In 2005, Vital Smarts published *Silence Kills* in which it documented the results of a study it conducted aimed at discovering how often clinicians (nurses, physicians, and technicians) actually spoke up when faced with situations of incompetence, poor teamwork, lack of support, work-arounds (i.e., not following policy or process), and disrespectful or abusive behavior (Maxfield 2005). Its findings were shocking: only 1 in 10 health care practitioners actually spoke up in these situations; the rest remained silent. How could this be? Of course we knew from previous studies that communication breakdowns are very common in health care, but to suggest that 90 percent of clinicians remain silent is attention-grabbing, and extremely concerning.

A nursing director relayed the following story that she witnessed in an operating room environment:

*One of the attending surgeons had a habit of talking to some of the nurses in a belittling tone (or at least that's how he was perceived).*

*He would throw out an insult or make a derogatory comment about their work, and seemingly think nothing of it. One nurse in particular was deeply troubled (and offended) by this behavior, as she felt she was frequently on the receiving end of these comments. Yet she never took the step to say something to the surgeon—she always just took it, and silently suffered. She was fairly introverted and quiet, so to confront the surgeon must have felt incredibly uncomfortable. She spoke with me a few times about her concerns and I always encouraged her to confront him, but she just didn't feel comfortable—and perhaps was worried about retribution. One day the surgeon made a comment to this nurse, which she interpreted as being unfairly critical of her competence as a nurse. She looked at the surgeon and said, "Ouch." He was startled, looked at her, and said, "What did you say?" She repeated herself: "Ouch. When you say those words to me, it hurts." This story has a good ending. The surgeon was genuinely surprised that his comments had had that effect on her; he had meant the comments to be humorous jabs and not to be taken personally. He apologized profusely and promised to watch himself in the future. And the nurse gained confidence that she could in fact speak up without facing harsh consequences. It was a good lesson for all of us.*

We recognize that there is a bit of a risk in sharing this story in that it further perpetuates the stereotype of inappropriate surgeon behavior in the operating room (OR). Certainly there are examples of all of the professions speaking inappropriately, but we felt this was a particularly poignant story with a strong lesson. We frequently choose not to speak up because of fear. Fear that the relationship will be damaged, or fear that the other person will become defensive and retaliate against us, fear that in the long run nothing will change, so why invest all of the emotional energy? The list goes on. And yet, as this story illustrates, if we are mindful of how we surface our concern, it is entirely likely that the other person will respond positively. Or at least the behavior will stop. A favorite quote of ours is: "When you name the game, the game ceases to exist."

Additional cases have been made for the importance of creating psychological safety. Building on the recent research conducted by Google on its internal teams (Duhigg 2016), where psychological safety was determined to be the key contributor to team performance, Drs. Jessica Wisdom and Henry Wie contend that the health care community can also apply these same lessons (Wisdom and Wei 2017). Many health care leaders are also familiar with resources such as *Crucial Conversations*, *Difficult Conversations*, and *Getting to Yes*, which provide specific skills for creating the conditions of psychological safety. Likewise, many also have experience with team training programs such as TeamSTEPPS, which focuses on building specific skills and knowledge in the areas of leadership, situation monitoring, communication, and mutual support. What all of these resources have in common is advocacy for creating a climate where team members feel safe to speak up and offer their perspective.

While all of these resources make strong cases as to the benefits of psychological safety, it is a lot to take in and it can be difficult for leaders to know where to begin. Therefore, based on our own experiences working with health care leaders and teams, as well as our familiarity with the previously mentioned resources, we would like to focus on the following core skills to create psychological safety:

- Suspend assumptions
- Establish a mutual goal
- Practice inquiry
- Empathy

## Suspend Assumptions

To fully understand what it means to suspend our assumptions, we first need to understand the concept of attribution error (sometimes referred to as fundamental attribution error or attribution of intent). The human brain does not like gaps. When we perceive gaps in a situation or an event, we rush to fill those gaps with our own speculations or assumptions about what must have actually happened.

Likewise, when we experience behavior from another person that does not match our expectations, or that disappoints us, we frequently (very frequently, in fact) make assumptions about the other person's true intentions. Consider driving on the freeway and someone in another car suddenly cuts in front of you, causing you to have to hit your brakes to stop from rear-ending them. Think about your first reaction (well, your first reaction after you have slowed your car down and avoided an accident!). Commonly we vent our frustration or anger at the other driver—"What were you thinking!" we yell. "You're crazy, insane, don't you realize you almost killed us all? You're an idiot!" And maybe we would throw in a few more choice words for good measure. And in one sense, aren't we justi-fied in our outburst? After all, this other person almost caused a serious accident that could have resulted in injuries.

But something else is also going on here: we begin to make fundamen-tal assumptions about the other driver's intentions. This person places no value on their own life or that of others, we may tell ourselves. Or perhaps we believe that they are irresponsible and reckless human beings and must behave this way all the time. Or maybe we believe this other driver sin-gled us out from dozens of other cars on the freeway and, at that precise moment, chose to cut us off, intentionally freaking us out and ruining our morning (especially if it caused our coffee to spill).

Here's another example: a physician and a patient care coordinator (PCC) on a diabetes unit were paired together and had been working together for several months. At some point a misunderstanding occurred that resulted in the two of them avoiding each other entirely, not speak-ing at all, for several months. The impact of this was felt by their patients and by their team members. When each of them was interviewed by an organization development consulting team called in to assist with the problem, the comments were fascinating. The PCC was confused by the physician's behavior and was also convinced the doc didn't like her, thought she was incompetent and was out to ruin her career. The physician also felt confused, and interestingly believed that the PCC was trying to get him fired by going to management with false stories about his behavior.

Of course neither assumption was correct, but in the heat of the battle, none of that mattered. Each was entirely convinced of their inter-pretation and also believed there was no way out of the predicament. In other words, they treated their assumptions as complete truth. And when we believe something that staunchly, it can be very difficult to move us off of our position, even when presented with alternative or contradictory data or facts.

So what is the fix for this, especially if it is so ingrained in us? A good place to start is to first recognize our reaction for what it is—an interpretation of events that is incomplete. Suspending our assumptions can help us to reengage the cognitive part of our brain, making it easier to consider alternative interpretations.

We all have our biases, opinions, and beliefs about how the world really works, and these have been shaped over the course of our lives by our upbringing, cultural background, education, religious beliefs, personality traits, and so on. The practice of suspension does not ask us to give up any of these beliefs (although it may be necessary for us to sometimes question and explore more deeply why we do in fact hold these beliefs), but rather allows us to set these beliefs, values, and perspectives off to the side, literally suspending them. And it is during that moment of suspension that we are able to be more fully present in the moment and actually see things without bias (or at least limited bias) and to consider other possible perspectives and interpretations.

In his book, *Man's Search for Meaning*, Viktor Frankl invites us to own our emotional responses and interpretations of events. He states, "You can take everything away from a human being except one thing: our ability to choose our response to any given situation or set of circumstance. That can never be taken away." He called this our *ultimate freedom* (Frankl 1985).

## Establish a Mutual Goal

Having a clear, common, articulate purpose can help unify people. In fact, when teams are asked to reflect on successful team experiences, having a common, mutual goal always makes the list—without exception. The question is what can leaders do to ensure this step is never missed, and that the goals are frequently revisited to ensure alignment?

An underlying concept of the team training program TeamSTEPPS (King et al. 2008)[1] is that of having a "shared mental model." When team members have this shared mental model, they are clear about their work,

---

[1] The TeamSTEPPS curriculum is available through Agency for Healthcare Research and Quality (AHRQ); the link to its website is: https://ahrq.gov/teamstepps/about-teamstepps/index.html

priorities, roles, and responsibilities. Teams that use the TeamSTEPPS methodology will frequently check each other by saying, "We don't have a shared mental model right now. What do we need to do to get on the same page?" In this context, the language and terms are known, so team members do not act defensively to this statement. They do not take it personally, and instead treat it for what it is, a realization that they need to get clear about their purpose. The environment still feels safe, and the team members can simply have a conversation about the perspectives they have and how to align around a common purpose.

The field of dialogue also calls out the importance of creating mutual purpose. Once, when working with the leadership team of a medical simulation center to create a strategic plan, it was immediately recognized that they had never fully articulated their core purpose, their reason for existence. The operation was relatively young (10 to 12 years old) and had experienced fairly significant growth and change. Working with the team to first clarify and articulate their purpose became the first order of business. The conversations they had were enlightening and helped them coalesce their multiple frames and perspectives, into a single, agreed upon purpose statement. This served to make the rest of the strategic planning process move more smoothly, because the purpose statement served as their touchstone.

Some important steps leaders can take to ensure mutual purpose exists are:

- Ask questions of team members to test for goal alignment— do they have a shared mental model?
- Ask, "What is it that binds us together in this effort? What do we have in common?" In health care, it will almost always center around the patient.
- When it is evident that team members are working at cross-purposes, call it out explicitly; then engage the members in a conversation about the goal they are trying to accomplish.

## Practice Inquiry

A key practice of exceptional leaders is to ask really good questions. This does not come naturally to us in health care; we are trained to diagnose, make decisions quickly, and solve problems. In fact it is this "problem solving nature" of ours, along with working in an environment that is very fast-paced, that prevents us from taking the time to explore how others are seeing an issue or a situation. Therefore, a simple practice that health care leaders can adopt is to start asking others questions—inquire into how they are seeing things, what their experiences have been, and what ideas they might have about a challenge or problem.

This is not to say that leaders (or anyone else for that matter) should not share their views, opinions, and perspectives. The problem is we unconsciously practice this advocacy of our own ideas and opinions routinely, and usually forget to ask others what they are thinking. The authors of *Crucial Conversations* refer to this as balancing advocacy with inquiry (Patterson 2002).

Kurt shares: Frequently, when I am conducting workshops on improving dialogue skills I will hold my arms out to either side, like a scale. I will ask the participants, "Think of our western society for a moment. If my right hand represents advocacy of my own ideas, and my left hand represents inquiry, asking others what they think, which way would you tilt me?" Without fail, they tell me to tilt to the right, toward advocacy. This simple activity reinforces the point that we are generally predisposed to offer our own opinions, and rarely do we explore others' perspectives.

Steven Covey popularized the notion of "seek first to understand," and that if we genuinely make an effort to learn how another is seeing the situation, it will strengthen relationships and result in better outcomes (Covey 2014). More recently, renowned MIT professor Edgar Schein published *Humble Inquiry*, in which he explores in-depth the practice of inquiry (Schein 2013).

Key elements to highlight:

- Make inquiry a habit—notice your own tendencies and create action triggers to help you ask questions first.
- Ask open-ended questions so you can learn what people are really thinking.
- Pay attention to your body language, your nonverbal cues— lean forward, nod, demonstrate your interest, take notes, repeat back what you hear, and summarize.

None of this is rocket science and most of us have heard this before. But it does require discipline—serious discipline. And leaders need to create and hold a container in which this type of communication can occur and thrive.

## Empathy (Your Ace in the Hole)

*Empathy is emptying our mind and listening with our whole being.*
—Marshall Rosenberg

A physician acquaintance of ours had volunteered to organize a bike ride in Oregon that required, among other things, coordinating parking at the start of the ride for the participants. The ride started in a small town and parking options were limited. As it turned out, many of the participants parked along a street that also housed several small businesses, including a restaurant. The physician happened to walk by the restaurant and the owner was out front and visibly upset. He was complaining that the cars belonging to the bicycle riders had taken all of the parking spaces and that his regular customers would have no place to park. Our colleague apologized to the owner and asked what he could do to make it right, perhaps offer him some money for the inconvenience. At that point the owner became irate: "I don't want your money! You think I want your money? You think you can just give me some cash and it makes everything all right?" Our colleague immediately sensed the shift, as well as his mistake. At this point he changed his approach and said to the owner, "You're absolutely right. I should not have made this presumption. It must be incredibly frustrating for you to arrive here and see that all of the parking spots in front of your store are taken." The owner calmed a little and said, "This is a small town, and we don't get a lot of customers. When you come in here and take up our spaces, it has an impact."

Our colleague told the owner he was sorry about this significant inconvenience and asked if he could at least buy him a cup of coffee. They went inside and sat down at a table and continued to talk, our colleague learning more about the owner and how he had started his business, and how proud he was of his work. A little later our colleague asked the owner if he would be willing to join their volunteer board. They didn't have any community members and it would be incredibly helpful if they had a local voice involved in their planning. The event had grown significantly over the years, and they simply had failed to consider the impact on the community as a whole. The owner enthusiastically agreed and a partnership was formed.

Empathy is truly an underutilized skill, and a real difference maker in creating a safe environment. We often refer to empathy as "our ace in the hole" when conversations or interactions start to go south (or sideways, as a good colleague, Michele Hamilton-Lane likes to say). Empathy is a concept we are all familiar with, but unfortunately not very good at practicing—or at least not as good as we think. Daniel Goleman believes empathy may be the most important skill for enhancing our emotional intelligence and making social connections with others (Goleman 1995). He also believes we are inherently poor at practicing empathy; the paradox is that most of us believe we are quite good at empathy. We would like to challenge that mindset.

The late Marshall Rosenberg devoted much of his adult life to practicing and teaching others the skill of empathy. His book *Nonviolent Communication: A Language of Life* devotes two chapters to the practice of empathy, but it appears consistently throughout the entire body of work, speaking to the importance he placed on it (Rosenberg and Chopra 2015).

When I ask participants in my leadership workshops to describe or define empathy, what I generally hear are statements such as putting yourself in someone else's shoes, seeing the situation from another's perspective, and there is quite often confusion between sympathy and empathy. When the participants are then presented with scenarios and asked to write out an empathic response, 95 percent of the responses are not empathic (at least not as defined by Rosenberg). So what then is this so-called ace in the hole that can rescue us from getting sucked into a downward spiral of conflict?

In its simplest form, empathy (as described by Rosenberg) invites us to acknowledge the emotion another person is experiencing and to seek to understand the unmet need that lies behind that emotion. We offer the following practices (along with the strong encouragement to read the resources listed at the end of the chapter).

Go to the balcony—imagine you are in a room full of people engaged in very lively conversation, perhaps even heated conversation. How do you react? Generally our tendency is to get completely absorbed in the conversation, and can even become emotionally attached to the content. Now imagine you remove yourself to a balcony that looks down upon the floor where all the people are gathered. How does the scene change? What are you more apt to notice now? Bill Ury is the first we are aware of to use this metaphor (Ury 1991), and we find it to be incredibly useful. This act is about changing our perspective, and the image of going to a balcony that both removes us from the immediate situation and also results in new observations can be powerful. Empathy is about getting out of ourselves so that we can better understand what is going on for the other person.

- Identify and acknowledge the emotion—we, as humans, actually have a very limited vocabulary to describe the emotions we experience. This is unfortunate.
- Understand the unmet needs of others—as discussed earlier, we experience strong emotions when we have needs that aren't being met. According to Rosenberg, we are often unaware of these needs because they are deep-seated.

One would think that those who have committed their working lives to the health care profession would all have a natural inclination toward empathy. Of course our own personal experiences, whether as patients in our health care systems, or working with others within the profession, do not necessarily support this. Or perhaps we encounter a health care provider who demonstrates empathy with her patients, but not with her coworkers. In fact, it may actually be possible that we all believe we are better at empathy than we really are.

For our purposes, we wish to highlight the importance of leaders practicing empathy because of the significant positive impact it can have on the team. Rosenberg describes empathy as the ability to acknowledge the emotion of another person, and to then understand the unmet need that lies behind that expression of emotion (Rosenberg and Chopra 2015). For example, if a team member makes a mistake that impacts others on the team, emotions they express could include distress, anxiety, worry, fear, and sadness. Being able to observe and sense these emotions in the team member is the first step. Next, we need to try to understand what unmet need lies behind the expressed emotion. At this point we also need to realize that we are, in effect, making an educated guess. What needs might this team member have based on the expressed emotions? A sample of possible needs include: being seen as competent in their job, to make a valuable contribution to the team and its work, and to feel supported by the other team members.

If the leader, or any other member of the team, is able to make an expression of empathy ("You seem upset and worried. Are you concerned the team is questioning your capabilities, and you want to know that we still support you?") it is highly likely that the team member will feel heard and understood, and will then be more likely to speak up and talk more about the event.

The "equation" we suggest for leaders, both to use themselves and also when coaching others, is:

$$\text{Strong emotions} = \text{unmet needs}$$

Here are a few barriers that can impede empathy, followed by some tips for practicing more empathy:

Barriers to Empathy:

- Problem solving—we get focused on offering solutions, when what the other person is really needing is to be heard.
- Empathy = agreement—we worry that if we show empathy toward someone, that equates to agreement.
- Our judgmental nature—we are hardwired to make judgments about others; often these initial judgments are wrong (refer back to the fundamental attribution error in Chapter 3).
- Confusing sympathy with empathy—empathy statements begin with word "you," as in "You must be feeling _____." Empathy attempts to reflect back to the person what is going on for them. Sympathetic statements begin with word "I," as in "I am saddened by your loss." The speaker is attempting to state their reactions, thoughts, or emotions.

Empathy Tips:

- Humanize the other person; ask yourself: "Am I seeing this person as another human being, who has wants, needs, hopes, fears, and dreams, just like me? Or am I seeing this person as merely an object or an obstacle that is standing in my way?"
- Be fully *present*. This requires that we not bring anything from the past into the conversation. Martin Buber says, "This is the most powerful gift one person can give to another."
- Connect to what's *alive* in the other person; get in touch with their "life energy" by connecting to their feelings and needs. This means we have to totally "tune in" to the other person and move away from problem solving and engaging in "intellectual understanding." Marshall Rosenberg refers to it as, "emptying the mind and listening with our whole being."
- Try using the phrase, "Are you feeling (x) because you're needing (y)?"
- One way to make sure the person has said all they want to say is to use the phrase, "Is there more you'd like me to hear before I respond to what you're saying?" This lets the other party know we are engaged and interested in what they have to say, and it demonstrates respect by offering to take more time to listen.
- Work to understand what the other person is feeling and needing before offering correction. This empathic connection often makes the task of offering the correction much easier, both for you and for the receiver.

*Source:* Handout from Empathy Workshop: Chuck Pratt and Kurt O'Brien

# In Summary

Clearly, health care leaders need to be tuned into how psychologically safe their team members feel to speak up and offer different perspectives or concerns. Of course the challenge lies in how to do this effectively. It is our hope that the strategies outlined here (suspending assumptions, establishing a mutual goal, practicing inquiry, and using empathy) will help leaders take definitive steps to improving the culture of psychological safety within their own teams, and thus positively impact the experiences of the patients and families they serve. The ability to foster an environment of psychological safety will also allow teams to be more flexible and adaptive as they respond to a constantly changing environment; we will examine this idea of adaptability more closely in the next chapter.

## End of Chapter Reflective Questions

- How do you, as a leader, determine whether or not your team members feel safe to speak up? What methods do you employ?
- What steps have you taken to increase psychological safety among your team? How do you know whether these steps are effective?
- How could you implement the ideas presented in this chapter with your team? Create an action plan for you to follow.

## References

Covey, S.R. 2014. *The 7 Habits of Highly Effective Families*. St. Martin's Press.

Duhigg, C. 2016. "What Google Learned from its Quest to Build the Perfect Team." *The New York Times Magazine*, 26.

Frankl, V.E. 1985. *Man's Search for Meaning*. Simon and Schuster.

Goleman, D.P. 1995. *Emotional Intelligence: Why It Can Matter More than IQ for Character, Health and Lifelong Achievement*. New York: Bantam Books.

King, H.B., J. Battles, D.P. Baker, A. Alonso, E. Salas, J. Webster, L. Toomey, and M. Salisbury. 2008. TeamSTEPPS™: Team Strategies and Tools to Enhance Performance and Patient Safety.

Maxfield, D. 2005. *Silence Kills: The Seven Crucial Conversations for Healthcare*. VitalSmarts.

Patterson, K. 2002. *Crucial Conversations: Tools for Talking When Stakes are High*. Tata McGraw-Hill Education.

Rosenberg, M., and D. Chopra. 2015. *Nonviolent Communication: A Language of Life: Life-Changing Tools for Healthy Relationships.* PuddleDancer Press.

Schein, E.H. 2013. *Humble Inquiry: The Gentle Art of Asking Instead of Telling.* Berrett-Koehler Publishers.

Ury, W. 1991. *Getting Past No: Negotiating in Difficult Situations.* Bantam.

Wisdom, J., and H. Wei. 2017. "Cultivating Great Teams: What Health Care Can Learn from Google." Retrieved from http://catalyst.nejm.org/psychological-safety-great-teams

# CHAPTER 4

# The Adaptive Team

*Adaptive capacity allows leaders to respond quickly and intelligently to constant change. It is the ability to identify and seize opportunities. It allows leaders to act and then evaluate results instead of attempting to collect and analyze all the data before acting.*

—(Wong 2004)

*Improvisation is the ability to create something very spiritual, something of one's own.*

—Sonny Rollins

If you happen to be a jazz enthusiast, you are likely tuned in to how the best jazz bands seamlessly riff off of one another, adapting the music in the moment to create one effortless sound. While it may seem effortless to us as listeners and observers, it actually takes skill and coordination. The beauty of improvisational jazz is that the musicians create something new and unique, without having to start entirely from scratch. As the website apassion4jazz.net indicates, "The structure is flexible so that the soloist may venture in various directions depending on the inspiration of the moment. A jazz musician is creating spontaneous art every time he or she plays music."

This notion of having a "flexible structure" is an important concept for health care leaders and teams. To be adaptive is not to say there should not be structure, consistency, or standardization. What it does mean is that leaders and teams must be equipped to first diagnose the situations, and then respond to the changing environment in as fluid a way as possible. Klein and Pierce liken adaptability to a team being dexterous, which in turn allows the team to have the capacity to improvise as events warrant (Klein and Pierce 2001).

In fact, the best health care teams already do this. Consider code response teams that come together to provide immediate assistance in cardiac cases, or the ED team that must quickly move from one case to the next, adapting to each unique situation as it presents itself. Certainly, procedures, protocols, and algorithms exist to assist these clinicians, but they also must rely on their intuition and experience, taking in information, properly assessing the situation, communicating effectively, while simultaneously being ready for the situation to change at a moment's notice. This is the nature of many of our teams in health care, and it is not just limited to our clinical settings. Administrative teams face similar challenges as the environment continues to change rapidly. Consider the Affordable Care Act and the myriad changes it has brought about—accountable care networks, reimbursement based on value rather than volume, transformational care efforts, the Triple Aim, and so on. And the stakes are getting higher. The ability of leaders to appropriately diagnose and respond to these challenges is paramount.

Because of this constantly changing environment that is so prevalent today, our teams need rigorous and relevant models that assist them with navigating change. This chapter will introduce health care leaders to the most current, cutting-edge models that deal with leading and adapting to change. The fields of complexity science and developmental psychology will form a foundation of practical tools that can be used to more fully engage teams in identifying and responding to challenges. Examples include the use of liberating structures (LS) (practices that engage team members in creative ways and at the same time increase shared ownership and appreciation for different perspectives), and a model of developmental readiness, where team members identify their motivation and ability to learn, grow, and develop.

Strategies to help teams be more adaptive:

- Assess and understand the environment.
- Assess the nature of the challenges they are facing (technical or adaptive).
- Try new things—practice experimentation.
- Generate engagement at all levels.
- Foster a culture of learning and development.

## Assess and Understand the Environment

As has already been discussed many times, the health care environment continues to evolve and change at a breathtaking pace. The challenge is that leaders and teams have not experienced this degree of complexity, and many are not adequately prepared to respond to it. Rapid technological changes, attempts to integrate disparate electronic medical records (EMRs), public reporting of quality, safety, and satisfaction results all make for a world that is much more complex for today's health care leaders and teams. And what's more, as the degree of complexity and uncertainty continues to rise, the frustration of these players mounts.

As a first step to increasing the ability to respond to this ever-changing environment, we recommend conducting an environmental scan, a practice that has long been used in traditional strategic planning efforts to help organizations more fully understand the factors (internal and external) that could impact their future activities and actions. When conducting an environmental scan, it is advantageous to include all members of the team in order to gain as many different perspectives as possible. Examples of factors to assess from the perspective of the internal environment include: policies and procedures, changes in senior leadership, adoption/implementation of new technologies, cross department interactions, finances, and so on. Examples of factors to assess from the external environment include: regulatory changes and trends, the political climate, research and development, social trends, and so on.

In fact, there is evidence that suggests the more an organization is in tune with its surrounding environment, the greater its longevity as the organization tends to be "more in harmony" with its environment (De Geus 1997), and is better able to respond and react to changes.

The importance of assessing and understanding one's own environment is no less important today; what has changed is that we need to be much more discerning about the lenses we use to view this complex, multicolored environment. If we only consider the environment based on our own biases and views of the world (what we know to be true), we will undoubtedly miss something. And that something we miss could have a vital impact on the team or organization down the road, not to mention the patients we care for.

So what can we do to expand, or broaden, our perspective in this area? Earlier in Chapter 3 we introduced the principle of suspending assumptions, as well as the metaphor of "going to the balcony" (Ury 1991); we would now like to highlight this concept in more detail as it applies to assessing and understanding one's environment.

Essentially, the idea of going to the balcony involves removing oneself from the attachment of being "in the thick of it all." Consider a crowded networking event in a large conference hall where dozens of people are mingling and getting to know one another. What is your experience like as a member of this moving throng? Likely, you are focused on what is right in front of you—the person you have just met and the conversation you are engaged in. Your brain is also likely forming immediate impressions of these other people, and determining whether you would like to continue speaking with them because you have mutual interests and you find them fascinating, or whether you should move on to the next person.

Now imagine there is a small balcony located 30 feet above the conference room floor. You decide to make your way to the balcony to get a break from the networking. When standing at the rail of the balcony and looking down on the event, what happens to your perspective? What shifts for you? What do you see now that you couldn't see before? This is the nature of "going to the balcony." It requires a deliberate and specific shift in mindset. It forces us to ask the question, "How can I see this differently? How can I change my perspective?"

On the surface this may seem like a simple exercise. In our experience, it is anything but that. Suspending our existing biases and beliefs is not easy at all. We tend to automatically default back to what is known and what is comfortable. Our biases remain prevalent. Of course the good news is that, while these biases do in fact exist, we are not beholden to them—we can make deliberate choices to act or behave in ways that free us up from our biases.

A good example of the inherent difficulty in shifting our perspective is the Harvard Implicit Association Test (IAT) (Greenwald et al. 2002; Greenwald, Nosek, and Banaji 2003). A group of educators and researchers from multiple institutions collaborated to create a battery of questionnaires to help us see where our actual unconscious biases lie. Do you associate women with career or family? Do you associate a photo of an African-American male with a positive or negative word? Having this knowledge increases our awareness of the biases that are actually at work, and gives us the opportunity to respond in new ways.

In his three decades plus of studying human development, Robert Kegan has hypothesized three main levels of adult development: the socialized mind, the self-authoring mind, and the self-transforming mind (Kegan and Lahey 2009, 2016). When we are at the level of the socialized mind, it is akin to being in the middle of the networking event (or dance floor, depending on your preference) and being emotionally and mentally connected to the other people you come into contact with. You are able to have engaging conversations, but it can be difficult to remove yourself from the content of the conversations. It can be easy to get sucked into what the other person is saying, contemplating your degree of agreement or disagreement.

With the self-authoring mind we find it easier to objectively assess the content of the conversation and perhaps consider (from a standpoint of curiosity) what biases, values, and belief systems may be informing the person's commentary and perspective. This type of thinking gets us closer to the balcony.

Advancing to the self-transforming mind gets us all the way to the balcony. Perhaps even beyond the balcony. We are able to see things with new clarity and to consider a perspective we would have previously been blind to. We are able to both assess and understand our biases and filters, examining them in a more objective way. It is this level of self-assessment that frees us up to make different choices. As Kegan and Lahey put it, a self-transforming mind "is aware that what might make sense today may not make as much sense tomorrow" (Kegan and Lahey 2016).

In reality, we are never able to completely remove or dismiss our biases, for they are deeply ingrained. However, heightened awareness of our biases allows us to see things from a new perspective. Therefore, moving to the balcony while conducting an environmental scan truly allows us to consider the world around us (and what is consequently impacting us, or likely to impact us) from the broadest perspective possible.

Another methodology that can be useful when assessing the environment is to consider the environment through different frames, or categories. Examples of different frames include: political, regulatory, science, technology, social networking, communication, and so on. Asking people to pick a frame, researching what is going on in that area, and then reporting back to the group can be a useful way to accumulate a broad array of information about the various frames selected.

We have found that when working with teams, simply engaging them in a dialogue about what they see happening in their world (internally and externally), and the possible implications, serves to (1) diversify the perspective of the group and (2) create a shared understanding of what is happening around them.

## Assess the Nature of the Challenges

In Chapter 2, we focused on the importance of teams being able to learn, and we introduced the concept of adaptability. Dr. Ronald Heifetz and Marty Linsky of Harvard have introduced a leadership approach known as adaptive leadership, and it is something we all need to be paying greater attention to. One of the core tenants of Heifetz's model is being clear about the distinction between *technical problems* and *adaptive challenges* (Heifetz, Grashow, and Linsky 2009).

Technical challenges are known. We have proven methods, processes, tools, and approaches with which to tackle these problems, and we can be reasonably assured that our efforts will result in success. Examples of technical problems include installing a new piece of equipment, repairing existing equipment and instruments, refining a purchasing process, or generating a new report. Or as Heifetz would say, technical problems "live in people's heads and logic systems. They have clear-cut solutions and can be solved with knowledge and procedures already in hand" (Heifetz, Grashow, and Linsky 2009).

With adaptive challenges, things are not as straightforward. Solutions are not so readily available, or when we apply a solution that we think should work (because it worked before) it fails miserably and we aren't sure why. All of a sudden people don't know what to do, and it becomes easier to avoid the problem altogether, or impose a solution, even though we know it's only a band-aid solution. In these instances, new knowledge is required; new models, methods, and approaches must be considered. In other words, new learning is required here. Adaptive challenges tend to be

*Table 4.1  Technical vs. Adaptive challenges*

| Technical | Adaptive |
|---|---|
| Clear answers, minimal uncertainty | No clear answers, often high uncertainty |
| Straightforward, few big choices | Time consuming, difficult choices |
| Can be executed by individuals via clear/ precise instructions | Requires lots of conversations and execution by many |
| Focus on task | Focus on people and task |
| Linear, demands precision | Nonlinear, demands creative thought |
| Tends to run smoothly | Conflict, distress, and fear are common |

most prevalent when behaviors, values, and belief systems are challenged. Whenever people talk about the need to change the culture, you have an adaptive challenge on your hands. Examples include forming a new team, and implementing a new process that significantly changes how people have performed or behaved in the past. (See Table 4.1 for a comparison of adaptive and technical challenges.)

Heifetz argues that a significant leadership failure is addressing adaptive challenges as though they were technical problems. And of course, this makes sense. We are frequently creatures of habit and it is comfortable to use approaches that have worked in the past and that we therefore believe should work now. So the first step for leaders is to simply *recognize* this distinction between technical and adaptive challenges.

## Try New Things—Experiment

When a large outpatient specialty center decided to move to a new location and expand their operations, leadership also wanted to implement patient self-rooming. The various clinics had never used this process before and everyone was worried that their patient satisfaction scores (which were excellent) might suffer as they implemented this new process. After having additional conversations they decided on the strategy of enlisting their patients as participants in "trying out this new process." When a patient arrived to check in at the center, they were offered the opportunity to participate in the new, innovative process of self-rooming. The front desk staff would explain the new process and ask the patient if they would be willing to give it a try, and to also provide feedback so the clinic staff could continue to refine and improve the process. The patients were also told they did not have to participate if they did not wish to, and in such cases a medical assistant would room the patient.

Using this approach accomplished several things: it allowed the staff to turn control over to the patient, so the patient didn't feel put upon by the change, and it put the staff at ease since they knew the patient could decline if they so desired. Ultimately, many of the patients ended up participating in the new process, and the clinic was able to continue to make improvements.

In high school science classes many of us experienced lab sessions where we had the chance to actually see the theories we were learning applied in an actual experiment. It was a chance to try something, see how it worked, and then learn from that process. We need to create more opportunities for our teams to try new things—to create and innovate. Leaders can set the stage for trying new things by encouraging teams (and individuals) to try a small test of change. We sometimes mistakenly believe that trying something new, or experimenting, requires a massive change. This is not the case at all. In their book, *Immunity to Change*, Robert Kegan and Lisa Lahey encourage individuals to conduct small experiments and then see what happens. It is akin to dipping a toe in the water, rather than jumping in the deep end (Edmondson 2012; Kegan and Lahey 2009).

## Generate Engagement at all Levels

The thing about adaptive challenges is that they do not lend themselves well to a single person working on them. You need to get others involved—you need to *mobilize* others to think and act. This is a core element of Heifetz's approach. The practice of LS, created by Keith McCandless and Henry Lipmanowicz, offers us unique ways in which to engage people at all levels of an organization, but the strategies work especially well with teams. The tagline on their website (liberatingstructures.com) reads, "Including and unleashing everyone." Their approach is grounded in complexity science and places a premium on self-organizing, learning processes. McCandless and Lipmanowicz argue that most of the structures and organizing principles present in our organizations today typically do not generate engagement and open dialogue. Oftentimes leadership or a committee has come up with "the solution" that is then imposed on the rest of the group or organization. While the intentions of these leaders and committees are noble, the result of these actions often leads to resistance, doubt, or apathy.

> *Liberating Structures introduces tiny shifts in the way we meet, plan, decide and relate to one another. They put the innovative power once reserved for experts only in the hands of everyone.*
> —(Liberating Structures 2016)

McCandless and Lipmanowicz created 33 LS (sometimes referred to as microstructures) and they are all available on their website and can be used free of charge (they only ask that users recognize their work). Clicking on a given structure provides a detailed description and purpose of the structure, along with guidance on how to actually use it. Let us share an example of LS in practice to illustrate.

An executive master of healthcare administration (MHA) student used the LS "TRIZ" to engage her ER team in examining why it was taking so long to transfer patients from the ED to the OR for the surgical procedure (in many cases, it was over an hour, and the surgeons were getting extremely frustrated). The premise of TRIZ is to get a group to consider all of the different ways they could make their initiative or project fail— yes, fail. Teams generally enjoy this process as they are free to consider all of the plausible, including what can seem downright ludicrous, ways their work could be sabotaged. But the process does not end here, in fact it is at this point that the heat gets turned up a bit. Participants are then asked to review the behaviors on their list, and call out any that they actually engage in. This is a critical moment in the process, and there is often a short period of silence until a brave soul will declare, "Yes, I sometimes do that." It usually takes just one person to break the logjam, and then everyone (or almost everyone) joins in. Here is how the MHA student described her experience once she asked this question of her group:

> Then I turned it around. "Any of you ever do any of these things?" Silence filled the air, a few people shifted in their seats. So I started

off by saying, "Well, I know that I have been guilty of one or two of these myself." Here came the voices and acknowledgment of participation in our list of "not to do's." This was great, [and] we decided to delve even deeper and look at why we were doing these things and the list exploded. Some actions were intentional and others people were not even aware they were inadvertently participating in the no-no's.

This is a fantastic example of engaging a team in a creative way to address a problem. Rather than the leader developing "the" solution, the group owned the process and as a result the members were able to identify possible solutions and implementation strategies.

In speaking more with this student, she expressed how helpful it was to first diagnose the situation in terms of technical versus adaptive problems. By being clear she was dealing with an adaptive challenge, she recognized she would need to use a different approach to engage the team. In addition to applying the LS TRIZ, she also leveraged the change model Switch from the book by the same name, written by Chip and Dan Heath. She used specific elements of that framework (namely Script the Critical Moves, Find the Feeling, and Grow Your People) to allow the team to fully own the problem and generate the solutions. She was amazed at the energy that came out of the team as she facilitated the process, and the number of ideas generated was more than she imagined. The team established a goal of 45 minutes to transfer the patient from the ED to the OR. They tested their new process (think experimentation), tracking the results of each transfer. At the end of the two-week period, she brought the team back together to reveal the results (in a sealed envelope, no less) and discovered they had surpassed the 45 goal with an average time of 36 minutes. The team was thrilled, as were the surgeons.

A key element to this success story was the willingness of the student to take on the role of facilitator for the team. She was able to pay attention to process but, more importantly, her knowledge of these tools gave her a way to engage the members of her team in ways she had never before considered. The success of the effort speaks for itself.

The intent of this section was to provide an example of the power of involving the people closest to the work in both understanding the problem or challenge, and then generating solutions to test. In 2012 a group of researchers concluded an 18-month study of engaging front-line staff in generating solutions to significantly reduce hospital-acquired infections (HAIs) at five Canadian hospitals (Zimmerman et al. 2013). Using a combination of LS, as well as other employee engagement strategies, the researchers involved the clinical staff closest to the problem and saw improved results across the board. They named their approach FLO, front-line ownership, and published an essay outlining this approach. At the end of the study they observed that the rate of infection (measuring the combined organism rate) decreased by nearly half on the units involved in the FLO initiative. As a result, the authors of the study offered the following insight:

> The FLO approach acknowledges the elephant in the room, namely that front-line staff actually know what steps need to be taken to improve patient safety, but that they have not been engaged in a way that encourages them to become part of the solution (Zimmerman et al. 2013).

## Foster a Culture of Learning and Development

Clearly there are strong linkages between learning and adaptation. In fact we would argue that you can't have one without the other. Therefore, in order to have an adaptive team, as this chapter calls out as an important factor in leading health care teams, leaders need to pay particular attention to how they are creating the conditions for learning to thrive as part of the culture. In Chapter 2 we focused on the elements needed to help teams adopt a learning framework:

- Mindset
- Adaptability
- Positive deviance
- Getting comfortable with making mistakes
- Debriefing

We would now like to build on this thinking by addressing the cultural aspect of this work.

A close colleague of Kurt once stated, "Leaders own culture. And it is an irrevocable responsibility." This is a powerful statement and, if you believe it, carries many implications for today's health care leaders. So how does a leader (or collection of leaders) go about influencing the culture such that an environment of continuous learning and development exists and truly thrives? We offer the following thoughts on this topic.

Before proclaiming that you will create a learning culture, it would first help to understand the forces that prevent us from learning in the first place. Consider your own organization for a moment and note the barriers that exist to the occurrence of continual learning—items you might identify could include the following:

- Fear of admitting ignorance (concern of other people's impressions, covering up perceived inadequacies)
- Rewarded for having an answer
- A strong need to "be right"
- Not valuing the time it can take to engage in a learning process
- Criticism or negative judgment
- Downplaying the reality of a changing situation in the environment

(De Geus 1997; Kegan and Lahey 2016; Vogt 1995)

These factors have a strong influence on us and are present in many (if not most) health care organizations. Certainly there are pockets where one would not encounter these inhibitors, but by and large, we are challenged with these barriers. Amy Edmondson addresses this by stating that we need to "learn to learn from failure" (Edmondson 2012). To be clear, she is not glibly stating we need to merely learn from failure. She is saying we need to *learn* to learn from failure. The potential barriers to learning just listed act to counter learning from occurring. Therefore, we advocate for addressing these barriers head on, rather than hoping they will go away or that they do not exist. And we believe the best way to do this is by engaging teams directly in conversation about the barriers that exist to learning. Using strategies from LS can be a useful and productive way to call out and address these barriers. In fact, using the LS TRIZ could be one effective way to generate dialogue about barriers and what needs to be done to reduce or eliminate those barriers.

Kegan and Lahey provide the most current examples of efforts underway to create what they call "deliberately developmental organizations" or DDOs (Kegan and Lahey 2016). Without going into extensive detail here (we highly recommend reading their book), one of their key findings in studying three DDOs is that they were able to effectively blend, in a very intentional way, the work of the business (operations, processes, and outcomes) with individual development. In fact, Kegan and Lahey believe that the DDO framework may be the most important factor in responding to adaptive challenges (p. 6).

The bottom line is, if leaders commit to fostering a culture of learning, they need to be fully engaged and must model the behaviors they wish to see in others. It is not just about making learning a priority (framing, as Edmondson calls it (Edmondson 2012)), but also about making it relevant, engaging, rigorous, and fun. Some suggestions for creating a team learning culture include:

- Have each team member identify the aspects of themselves that they want to further develop.
- Have the team determine (through a facilitated process) how they can better focus on learning—this way the team owns it rather than feeling a process is forced upon them (this may also require the team to assess its own readiness to learn).
- Create opportunities to practice and then debrief how the practice went.
- Peer coaching—pair people up to coach each other on those aspects of their work or leadership they want to further develop (also see the LS Troika consulting as a possible methodology).
- Find ways to make the learning fun.

*The essence of learning is discovery through play.*

—*Arie DeGeus*

## In Summary

Building the adaptive capacity of your teams will be critical for thriving in today's complex health care environment, and we have offered but a small number of considerations. However, in our effort to share some of these strategies, we have been deliberate in tapping into what we consider to be some of the more current and leading-edge theories and models for creating adaptive teams. Certainly there are other models and perspectives out there—regardless of what strategies you choose to adopt, our main hope is that you do so in a deliberate way that engages people in meaningful ways.

Furthermore, by focusing on the activities of assessing the environment, determining the nature of the challenges you are facing, experimenting, generating engagement at all levels, and fostering a culture of learning, you will be creating the conditions for your team members to assume ownership for their work, which is the topic of the next chapter.

## End of Chapter Reflective Questions

- What steps have you taken (or will you take) to assess and understand your current environment? How will you involve your team in this effort?
- How can you further incorporate the practice of experimentation into the work of your team? Is there anything you are currently doing that would block this practice?
- Are you advocating buy-in or true ownership? How does your leadership practice need to change/evolve to generate higher levels of ownership?

## References

De Geus, A. 1997. *The Living Company: Habits for Survival in a Turbulent Environment*. London: Nicholas Brealey.

Edmondson, A.C. 2012. *Teaming: How Organizations Learn, Innovate, and Compete in the Knowledge Economy*. John Wiley & Sons.

Greenwald, A.G., M.R. Banaji, L.A. Rudman, S.D. Farnham, B.A. Nosek, and D.S. Mellott. 2002. "A Unified Theory of Implicit Attitudes, Stereotypes, Self-Esteem, and Self-Concept." *Psychological Review* 109, no. 1, p. 3.

Greenwald, A.G., B.A. Nosek, and M.R. Banaji. 2003. "Understanding and Using the Implicit Association Test: I. An Improved Scoring Algorithm." *Journal of Personality and Social Psychology* 85, no. 2, p. 197.

Heifetz, R., A. Grashow, and M. Linsky. 2009. *The Practice of Adaptive Leadership.* Boston, MA: Harvard Business School Publishing.

Kegan, R., and L.L. Lahey. 2009. *Immunity to Change: How to Overcome it and Unlock Potential in Yourself and Your Organization.* Harvard Business Press.

Kegan, R., and L.L. Lahey. 2016. *An Everyone Culture: Becoming a Deliberately Developmental Organization.* Harvard Business Review Press.

Klein, G., and L. Pierce. 2001. "Adaptive Teams." U.S. Army Research Laboratory sponsored report.

Vogt, E.E. 1995. "Learning Out of Context." *Learning Organizations: Developing Cultures for Tomorrow's Workplace*, pp. 293–303.

Wong, L. 2004. *Developing Adaptive Leaders: The Crucible Experience of Operation Iraqi Freedom.* Carlisle, PA: Strategic Studies Institute, US Army War College.

Zimmerman, B., P. Reason, L. Rykert, L. Gitterman, J. Christian, and M. Gardam. 2013. "Front-Line Ownership: Generating a Cure Mindset for Patient Safety." *Healthc Pap* 13, no. 1, pp. 6–22.

# CHAPTER 5

# Creating Ownership

One of the ultimate goals for a team is to have the ability to identify problem or challenge areas as they arise and to then self-correct. This is an extremely challenging undertaking, but doable. The previous four chapters lay the groundwork for the practice of self-correcting, which comes from adopting a learning mindset, fostering adaptive practices, and paying attention to the psychological safety of the team. When teams reach this state of self-correction, the degree of ownership can increase dramatically. In this chapter we wish to further explore the concept of ownership—what it is, how it differs from "buy-in," and how it can be an incredible source of leverage for your teams.

## Buy-in or Ownership?

It will first be helpful to be clear about what we mean by "ownership." In this context, we are talking about members of a team feeling that they have a very real stake in their work, that they have the ability to not just offer input, but to actually make change. This means that team members are involved in not just creating solutions, but also in the process of diagnosing or understanding the situation, event, challenge, or opportunity. This requires complete transparency so that all team members have access to the same information (McCandless and Lipmanowicz 2014).

Let us take a moment to make a distinction between ownership and buy-in. The term "buy-in" is frequently heard in our organizations, and is usually uttered by those in leadership roles. A new initiative or process is created and now the leaders need the rest of the team (or entire organization, for that matter) to buy-in to the initiative. When the term buy-in is used, it is with good intention. The leaders truly want others to adopt the new practice, methodology, process, or standard and they believe that, by communicating the new procedures, and the reasons behind them, and then putting in place specific policies or rules to follow, performance will follow. As leaders, we are then surprised when we encounter resistance in the trenches, or the new performance we are seeking does not materialize.

One of the significant challenges with wanting to create more owner-ship is that leaders are by default required to give up some level of control. One question then to ask yourself as a leader is are you interested in gar-nering compliance or do you want genuine ownership? If your aim is to have compliance (staff follow what they are told to do, or what is spelled out by leadership), then we would suggest you might not yet be ready to move toward full-on ownership.

Amy Edmondson relates a study she undertook demonstrating the impact a learning approach can have on how a new minimally invasive cardiac surgery procedure was introduced in 16 different hospital sys-tems. She discovered that those physician leaders who championed a learning approach and engaged their teams in the implementation pro-cess were far more successful with the full-scale implementation of the device (Edmondson 2012). The parallel we would draw is that, as a result of engaging in a learning process, these leaders actually generated a high degree of ownership. The new procedure typified an adaptive challenge—adopting it required changes in both technology/equipment and in how the team would have to function together. Narrowing her focus to four hospitals, two community hospitals, and two larger academic medical centers, she discovered that the way the leaders in each institution framed the adoption of the new procedure was the most critical factor in deter-mining successful implementation.

In the two hospitals that experienced successful implementation, the two surgeon leaders used an approach that framed the situation and was upfront about the challenges, and also fully engaged the surgical team in the adoption of the new procedure. Edmondson states: "To succeed in implementing change or transforming the way work is accomplished, leaders must frame their role in the project in ways that invite others to participate fully" (Edmondson 2012).

While we agree wholeheartedly with Edmondson's conclusions, we also believe that these leader actions result in a much higher degree of ownership on the part of the team, leader included.

Earlier we described how a large outpatient specialty center invited their patients to participate in testing out a patient self-rooming process. As the administrative director and the medical director prepared for the relocation to the new site, they planned and held a retreat for the entire clinic team where they were able to generate ideas for how to make the move to the new building more efficient, which also included modifying and re-designing processes. After the move was complete, the administrative director and his clinic leadership team conducted daily debriefs. The leaders of each clinic area (or pod, as they called them) would conduct the debrief and then send the results to the director, who would compile the feedback and use the information to conduct the next morning's brief. This way, the staff were able to see how their input and feedback directly helped to shape the next day's brief. They also held periodic all-staff meetings, but these were not structured as a typical meeting where people sat passively while others spoke "at" them. Rather, real situations were shared that were creating challenges for the clinic, and the participants were invited to help generate solutions, often working in small groups. These meetings were not all-day events, either; typically they lasted 90 to 120 minutes, but at the conclusion people felt they had actionable items to work on. Again, a sense of ownership and identity flourished as a result.

Henry Lipmanowicz (co-creator of LS) believes that anytime leaders start using the term "buy-in" it should be considered a warning sign that they are not doing enough to involve their people up front in the design or planning process and, as a result, they run the risk of alienating folks or inadvertently creating resistance.

Lipmanowicz also cautions against relying too heavily on adopting the so-called best practices from other institutions or consulting groups. The reason for his caution is that the practices in question were developed and implemented within a specific culture and context, and simply importing the practice in question may not work at all in your particular culture or context (McCandless and Lipmanowicz 2014). This is an interesting, if not somewhat heretical, assertion since seeking out best practices is a very common strategy in today's organizations, and one that is also touted by many consulting groups. Yet it also makes good sense, and perhaps helps to explain why so many change efforts fail to meet their stated objectives. He suggests three questions for leaders to address when considering importing a best practice:

Is the process designed to

- Impose the best practice?
- Achieve buy-in?
- Achieve ownership?

If the challenge is adaptive in nature, Lipmanowicz argues, it makes the best sense to follow a strategy aimed to achieve ownership. This supports Heifetz's mantra of mobilizing people and enabling them to do the work that is required to meet the challenge. Again, the process of diagnose, interpret, and intervene can apply here.

There is perhaps a risk that this notion of "mobilizing" others to create ownership could go the way of the empowerment craze of years ago. Empowerment, once hailed as a liberating process itself, was the approach that would allow people to take charge of their own direction, their own futures, in order to meet organizational goals. Today, empowerment is often considered an overused, overly optimistic buzz word that simply is not very evident in today's workplace. Our perspective is that empowerment may simply have gotten a bad rap. What was not well acknowledged during the heyday of empowerment is the critical role leaders play in creating the conditions that would make empowerment possible. It is also likely that many leaders viewed the empowerment movement as an affront on their own leadership responsibilities and could very well have been perceived as a loss of control.

In our minds it comes back to how does the leader see his or her role? We are arguing that in today's VUCA (volatile, uncertain, complex, ambiguous) world, leaders need to do more to create a learning environment, which in turn leads to teams being more adaptive to a changing environment, and ultimately engenders a higher degree of ownership on the part of team members—this is essentially the case we are attempting to make in this book.

## Generating Ownership

Going down the path of generating ownership is without a doubt a function of leadership. The previous three chapters provided detail about creating a learning environment, creating the conditions for psychological safety, and creating adaptive teams. All of the strategies presented can certainly contribute to creating ownership, but we would like to add the following strategies:

### Give the Work Back to the People Closest to the Work (also known as FLO)

We realize that we run the risk of this statement coming across as a mere platitude. If it were this easy, wouldn't we all be doing it? The reality is that leaders must make this a deliberate choice, and must be comfortable enough in their own skin to let go of control so that the front-line employees truly can take on the work—even if they resist it at first.

This is probably one of the biggest hurdles to overcome—you, as the leader, make the commitment to give the problem-solving work back to the staff, and yet they resist all of your attempts to do this. You hear comments like, "I thought it was your job to figure this out," or "I don't have time to figure this out, I'm busy with patient care. I couldn't possibly take the extra time it would take to work on this." The reality is that many of us have simply become used to depending on others (leaders) to make decisions for us, or to tackle the really tough problems.

Years ago, James Belasco and Ralph Stayer wrote a book entitled *Flight of the Buffalo*, where they addressed this very issue (Belasco and Stayer 1993). As leaders themselves, Belasco and Stayer discovered they had been responsible for taking on too many problems that could be solved at a local level, if employees were allowed to do so. They committed to a new approach that, when an employee brought them a problem to solve, rather than taking it on (as they had consistently done in the past) they would instead give it back to that employee by saying something like, "That sounds like a really interesting problem, Seth, what do you think you can do about it?"

The initial reaction from the individuals, as you might imagine, was shock, followed by resistance (or in some cases, resentment). Folks were simply not used to this new method, and so they responded the way we would expect folks to respond, by getting defensive and looking for ways to throw it back to the leader. But they held their ground, and soon they began to see results. Folks would go back, think about it, and eventually begin to come up with ideas on how to address the challenge they were facing. Pretty soon, they stopped coming by at all, because they were just jumping in working to resolve things. If they needed assistance, they knew they could ask for it, and then [authors] could consider taking a more active role.

Kurt actually put this strategy to use during his time in the Coast Guard. While managing a group at a large training center, and having read the *Flight of the Buffalo*, the next time one of his direct reports came to him with a problem to solve, he listened, and then asked the team member what he thought he should do about it. (He was incredibly worried that this approach would not work at all.) This response was not met with welcome arms. At least at first. But he held his ground and after a short while, this team member was telling him about the challenges that had come up and how he had dealt with them on his own. It completely changed the dynamics.

The point is to not come across as being dismissive, but rather supportive of the team members, entrusting them, really. And while some degree of resistance can be expected, sticking with the process is a must because, as soon as you fall back to old habits, the culture of dependence returns.

## Frame the Situation for Learning

We spoke quite a bit about what teams need to do to learn in Chapter 2; one of the leadership behaviors espoused by Amy Edmondson is that of "framing the situation for learning" (Edmondson 2012). Her point is that leaders need to take the necessary step of telling their team that the opportunities and challenges they face present a tremendous learning opportunity, and that they will do this learning together. Providing a supportive environment, while simultaneously challenging people to take initiative to solve problems, can seem like a paradox or a polarity. Rather than viewing this as an "either/or" choice, we see it as a "both/and" opportunity. Challenging people to solve a problem on their own and tap into their creativity does not mean we don't support them. The key is in how the challenge is presented, thus the focus on framing the situation as a learning opportunity.

## Use Liberating Structures to Engage People in New Ways

In the previous chapter we introduced you to the revolutionary engagement process of LS, and now we would like to reemphasize its use and importance in generating ownership. The value of using any of the microstructures is that they are fundamentally designed to get people engaged in talking about the real issues at hand. It is hard to opt out, because the design is all-inclusive—everyone has the ability to have a voice, which is, in one sense, the simplest definition of psychological safety. Another factor that makes the use of LS so compelling is that, for many (if not most) of the microstructures, they can be used with groups of any size. Scale is not important. Using them with a group of five is just as engaging as with a group of one hundred. What is more important is making sure you have the right people in the room. The ones whose voices really matter. The ones who have a stake in the process and the outcome.

Some of the specific microstructures that enable collaborative decision making include:

- 25 to 10 Crowd Sourcing
- Min Specs
- 15 percent Solutions
- Purpose to Practice (P2P)

We encourage you to experiment with the various microstructures as a way to further increase shared ownership. Start small and test one of them out. See what kind of results you get, and then adapt and build from there.

In today's team-based climates, creating ownership is critical and it is the leader's responsibility to set the stage for this to occur. We have presented several ideas here that contribute to the understanding of ownership, as well as the implementation, but at the end of the day it comes back to asking yourself, what are you really after?

To further illustrate the power of creating ownership, consider the following example from a University of Washington (UW) MHA student from an assignment on change and leadership:

*We were over two hours into the meeting, and things were buzzing during the break. People were having conversations about each of the themes and what came up in the discussions. It was clear that our culture was changing. That the focus on billing was counterproductive; we were at the wrong end of the spectrum. Everyone was doing this work because of the mission and clients we served, not to get rich. But because of the money we were starting to modify how we delivered our services, focusing on low-hanging fruit versus clients who needed the most support. It was hi-jacking our mission of serving clients and turning things into more of a numbers game, a competitive numbers game. Which in effect reduced our collaboration and put us into silos, which resulted in duplicated efforts and inefficiencies. People were also feeling the pressure and starting to crack under it. Feeling that we had to explore new revenue streams or a different way of operating because the current methods weren't sustainable. Overall, people felt like things needed to change.*

*The meeting ended with themes presented and discussed, needs and action items identified and prioritized, and staff members taking ownership of collectively working toward such via theme teams. In closing out the meeting via reflection and sharing thoughts on the day, quotes such as "we can't let this stop here," "we don't have to wait until next year to have another meeting, can we make it part of our monthly meetings?" displayed the group's energy behind the new approach and where we are headed. Our new approach was not only well received, it was adopted.*

This is an excellent example of how ownership can be enhanced using group process, and how leadership can set the stage.

## In Summary

In this chapter we have attempted to make the case for generating higher levels of ownership within teams, and the first step, in our minds, is to have a clearer understanding of the distinction between buy-in and ownership. Understanding this distinction allows leaders to be more mindful of what their goals truly are, and also causes them to pay better attention to which words they are using, and understand how people typically interpret these words.

Using strategies to get people engaged directly in the work makes a difference in generating the conditions for ownership to occur, so the leader needs to be aware of the actions taken to either help or hinder these conditions. In the next chapter, we examine what leaders can do to become more aware of how their own biases and worldview shape their actions and either encourage or inhibit engagement and ownership—and ultimately, team performance.

## End of Chapter Reflective Questions

- Think back to a time when you were given control (or autonomy) over a project or situation, and you seized the opportunity and tackled it with enthusiasm and optimism. A time when you were challenged, maybe even outside of your comfort zone, but you were fully engaged and felt fully supported by leadership. Reflect on that situation, recall what made this possible, and then think about how you can create similar circumstances with your own team.

- What opportunities exist within your work to "give the work back" to the people closest to the situation? Where have you avoided doing this in the past? What is a small step you can take to practice giving the work back?

## References

Belasco, J.A., and R.C. Stayer. 1993. *Flight of the Buffalo*. Dove Audio.

Edmondson, A.C. 2012. *Teaming: How Organizations Learn, Innovate, and Compete in the Knowledge Economy*. John Wiley & Sons.

McCandless, K., and H. Lipmanowicz. 2014. *The Surprising Power of Liberating Structures*. Liberating Structures Press.

# CHAPTER 6

# Your Role in the Team

*If your emotional abilities aren't in hand, if you don't have self-aware-ness, if you are not able to manage your distressing emotions, if you can't have empathy and have effective relationships, then no matter how smart you are, you are not going to get very far.*

—Daniel Goleman

Entire books have been written (and will continue to be written) on this topic; our goal is to highlight the importance of group dynamics, but doing so within the framework of creating high-functioning teams. As leaders work to create the conditions for their teams to function at a higher level, they must have the knowledge and skills to help the team navigate the complexity of group dynamics. But before the leader can take on this role, she or he must first know themselves and how they, at an individual level, impact the team. How do the leader's own preferences and biases influence the team? To what degree is the leader aware of their own values and belief systems and, more importantly, how these values and belief systems "show up," especially in high stress and high stakes situations? It is only after individual leaders have delved into these topics at a deeply personal level can they then take the next step of coaching and influencing their teams.

A department chair wished to improve the dynamics of his leadership team. The team was comprised of both physician and administrative leaders, and the group was struggling. Bickering and complaining were common occurrences, both during meetings and outside of meetings during the normal course of work. This type of behavior had become the norm, and the chair wanted to see better communication and more effective teamwork among colleagues. He asked an internal consultant for assistance in this endeavor.

The consultant met with the chair and each member of the team individually, and also observed several team meetings. At the conclusion of this interview and observation period, the consultant sat down with the chair to share her findings and to suggest a course of action. During the course of her interviews she found (as she suspected) that there were many differences of opinion and conflicting ideas on how to approach and solve problems, but she also discovered that the team was frustrated with the chair. They found him to be fairly quiet and unwilling to call people out on their bad behavior when it occurred. Furthermore, they felt the department was lacking direction. They wanted to know what they should be focusing on and how to get there. In short, they wanted stronger leadership.

The observation of the team meetings also bore this out. The consultant witnessed the chair sidestepping issues and cutting people off. To the consultant, he seemed unsure about how to handle the strong personalities on the team, and how to guide the group in working through their differences. When she brought this up in her meeting with him, he became uncomfortable. She suggested some strategies that were first aimed at enhancing his self-awareness of his own behaviors, before trying to work on fixing the team (in consultant speak this is known as "work on me first"). The chair was reluctant to follow this approach, and instead laid the blame at the feet of the team—"If they would just learn to get along and play nice, all of this would work out and everyone could get on with the work at hand." He told the consultant he would think about it, but never called her back.

Unfortunately, this is too often the situation. The leader fails to recognize their own contribution to the dynamics of the group and to commit to focusing on this first. As Chuck Pratt, an executive coach and consultant and close colleague, is fond of saying: "All relationships are co-created"; therefore, it is incumbent upon the leader to model strong self-awareness and to be willing to further their learning in this capacity if they hope for the team to change its behavior. There are several things leaders can do to strengthen their knowledge, awareness, and skills in this area.

## Understanding Personality Style and Preferences

All of us have lenses through which we see and experience the world. The problem is many of us can be unconscious of these views. Additionally, we all have preferences (which manifest in behaviors) that shape how we interact with the world around us. There are a multitude of models and tools available to help leaders gain clarity about their preferences and worldview: DISC, the Myers-Briggs Type Indicator (MBTI), Merrill's Personal Styles Inventory, and so on. Our intent is not to recommend one model over the other, but rather to encourage leaders to use *a model* to help them be clear about their preferences and how they shape their behavior. The key is in the learning, which goes back to our discussion in Chapter 2 about adopting a learning orientation (as opposed to just being focused on the goal or outcome).

For example, a leader may learn through the use of the MBTI that they have a preference for extroversion and can tend to insert their ideas into the group process before giving others an opportunity to speak up. Or perhaps a leader learns that they favor an analytic style (Merrill's Personal Styles) and is drawn to data and can tend to approach issues or challenges from a place of logic and can appear to others (unintentionally) as cold and calculating. If a leader is unaware of these tendencies, then how will it be possible to make different choices? So again, as a leader, choose at least one of the models available to help you learn about (or gain further clarity about) your own style and preferences. Not only does this assist with enhancing self-awareness, but it also helps create a common language for you to use with your team.

A clinic administrator and a medical director had been working together for about six months and they were experiencing some challenges in their working relationship. They had originally been very excited about their leadership collaboration but, as time had moved on, some frustrations had emerged for both of them. For example, the administrator became concerned that in certain meetings the medical director would suddenly jump into a situation and make a decision, when the administrator thought they had an agreement to consult each other first. The medical director felt that there were times when the administrator was questioning her ability to be a leader and, when this feeling arose, she would tend to take a stronger position on certain topics.

After meeting with the two leaders, it was clear that they both held each other in good regard, but they wanted some assistance working through these difficulties. The MBTI was administered and they learned that their type preferences were 180 degrees opposite—one had the preferences of ESTJ (extraversion-sensing-thinking-judging) and the other had INFP (introversion-intuition-feeling-perceiving) preferences. Once they were able to establish a common language using type, and better understand how their preferences showed up at work (especially during times of stress), their interactions improved (which also benefited their team).

This example provides a quick illustration of how understanding one's own preferences and style can improve self-awareness, understanding and appreciation of the other person, and positively impact results (i.e., team meetings).

Questions leaders should ask themselves when assessing their own personality style and preferences:

- How comfortable are you describing your process for making decisions?
- Are you clear about how you prefer to collect information about your external environment?
- When you experience challenges with another person, are you able to hypothesize about some of the different lenses through which you are interpreting your surroundings?

## Leveraging Emotional Intelligence

In this day and age, the leader who has not heard of emotional intelligence (EI) is rare. The number of leaders who understand the nuances of EI and actively engage in efforts to enhance/improve their own emotional intelligence may be much smaller. Since Daniel Goleman popularized EI with his book *Emotional Intelligence: Why It Can Matter More Than IQ* (Goleman 1995), dozens of leadership books and articles have been published with strategies on how to strengthen EI. Additionally, several assessment tools are now available that allow leaders to evaluate their emotional intelligence (these include self- as well as multi-rater assessments). From our perspective, the three assessment tools that have the best psychometric properties include: the BarOn Emotional Quotient Inventory (EQ-i) (now in version 2.0), the MSCEIT, and the Emotional Social Competency Inventory (ESCI) from the Hay Group.

While each model has its strengths, we will focus on four elements that we believe have the broadest impact: emotional self-awareness, interpersonal relationships (awareness of others), impulse control, and optimism.

## Emotional Self-Awareness

How aware are you of your own reaction when you experience disappointment? Are you aware of your trigger points, your so-called emotional hot buttons? And when those hot buttons are pushed, how do you react? And why do you believe you act that way when that trigger is pushed? These questions are all extremely relevant, certainly for all of us, but especially for leaders.

Emotional self-awareness is considered a foundational component of any leadership development program and it is incumbent upon all leaders to spend the necessary time considering their answers to these questions, and others like them. People often talk about the need to manage our emotions, but if we can't first identify our emotions when they occur, then managing them becomes an effort in futility.

Consider the following example: while going through an activity that posed questions very similar to those noted above, a nurse spoke of her frustration when a colleague wouldn't show up on time. She knew it was a hot button of hers, but she wasn't able to explain why it was a hot button. She bravely asked the rest of the participants to give her some insight and feedback on this. After asking some clarifying questions, it became clear that the nurse held a very strong personal value around being punctual, and if others didn't adhere to it, she would get angry. While reading this example here makes perfect sense to the rest of us, she literally was unable, in the moment, to connect her emotional response back to the deeply held value.

Steven Stein and Howard Book define emotional self-awareness as "the ability to recognize your feelings, differentiate between them, know why you are feeling these feelings, and recognize the impact your feelings have on others around you" (Stein and Book 2010). It is not uncommon for just the act of identifying our feelings to present challenges. Richard Davidson refers to this as being "Self-Opaque" (Begley and Davidson 2012). He states that people who have challenges of this nature are not necessarily denying their emotions, but rather they truly are not aware of the emotional indicators their body and brain are sending to them. Davidson's work focuses on understanding the connections between our brain—our neural pathways—and our emotions. For example, one's ability to easily detect their own heartbeat (or other physiological signals) is associated with higher degrees of emotional self-awareness.

Oftentimes, emotional self-awareness is associated just with recognizing and understanding your own emotional state. As noted earlier in the example with the nurse in the workshop, the ability to identify the cause of the emotions, and to understand how our emotional state may be impacting others, is just as important as the initial identification of the emotions. Once leaders are able to conduct this level of assessment for them, they are in a stronger position to then offer coaching to others to help them gain this same level of clarity (the practice of coaching will be presented later in this chapter).

Questions leaders should ask themselves when assessing their own level of emotional self-awareness:

- How are you able to identify your own emotional state? To what extent are you able to name the actual emotions?
- What are some of your own emotional hot buttons? How do you react when these buttons are pushed? Why do you believe you react this way? What are the consequences of your reaction?

## Interpersonal Relationships

Many research studies and literature reviews have noted how critical it is for leaders to engage in positive and productive interpersonal relationships, and it is apparent that a lack of ability to engage in effective interpersonal relationships is a very significant factor in derailing leaders' careers (Day 2001; Turner and Müller 2005; Van Velsor and Leslie 1995). And really, this should come as no big surprise. When conducting workshops and asking leaders to consider an exceptional leader whom they have personally known (or know), and to describe the characteristics and qualities of these leaders, the ability to build relationships and make connections with others is always mentioned (in fact, we would estimate that approximately 98 percent of the characteristics and qualities that are mentioned are directly related to emotional intelligence).

A new vice president (VP) had been hired at a medical group and the medical director was very much looking forward to working with his new partner. They had engaged in a very thorough vetting and interview process and this new VP had really shone. During the first several months they worked closely to develop a vision and corresponding plan for the medical group—a group that had been struggling over the past years. They fed off of each other's ideas, listened intently to one another, and were committed to doing whatever it took to help elevate the group to new levels. Eventually they presented the new vision and plan to the entire medical group, and it was received enthusiastically. As they continued to work together, their trust deepened and they reached a point where they felt they could almost read each other's thoughts.

Dr. Reuven Bar-On, the creator of the EQ-i inventory, speaks to the mutuality of the relationships, and this brief story is an excellent example of this concept [EQ-i technical manual]. That is, the extent to which both parties feel they benefit from the relationship (equal parts give and take), the stronger the bond. Stephen Covey's notion of the emotional bank account comes to mind: building trust and connection with another person places deposits in the emotional bank account of the other person (1989). The stronger the buildup in the account, the stronger the relationship and, when challenges or conflicts do arise, it is generally easier to work through them. This is the essence of Covey's win/win principle, where each party benefits from the experience, which fits very nicely with the concept of mutuality. (See Table 6.1).

Here is a brief list of key factors that contribute to mutually satisfying relationships:

*Table 6.1 Attributes that contribute to mutually satisfying relationships*

| | |
|---|---|
| • Kindness<br>• Empathy<br>• Compassion<br>• Listening intently (seek first to understand, in Covey's language) | • Attributing positive intent to others' actions<br>• Taking an interest in and supporting someone else's growth and development |

Actions leaders can take when assessing their own interpersonal relationships:

- Make a list of the most important relationships in your life, both at work and outside of work.
- Assess the current state of each of those relationships, what is working well, and what may need attention.
- Create a list of actions you can take to address any gaps or deficiencies.

## Impulse Control

*Anger in a leader can take on a special amplifying power among those led, simply because people pay so much attention to what they say and do.*

—Daniel Goleman relaying a statement from Ronald Heifetz during a conversation (Gyatsho, Goleman, and Richardson 2003)

All of us have heard stories of, or experienced firsthand, a leader who at some point "lost it" and became enraged, either yelling at the members of the team, throwing some piece of equipment, or in the worst cases making physical contact with a team member. In most cases, these outbursts can be linked back to some "trigger moment"; something changed with the situation, or was said that then caused the leader to react in such a way (this is not to excuse this type of behavior, but rather to understand where it is coming from).

Consider your own past reactions for a moment: can you recall a situation where you reacted a certain way—became angry, annoyed, or upset at a situation or at someone else—and upon further reflection you now wish you had responded differently? What was it that happened? Why do you think you reacted the way that you did? Given more time to think about the situation, would you have potentially reacted differently? Do you ever find yourself "leaping before you look" or have you ever received this feedback?

Impulse control is "the ability to resist or delay an impulse, drive or temptation to act" (Stein and Book 2010). The ability to manage our impulses ultimately has a significant impact on how others view our leadership effectiveness, and thus on whether they see us as credible or not. Not making rash decisions, the ability to remain calm and composed, and managing our emotions, especially anger and anxiety, are all hallmarks of effective impulse control (Stein and Book 2010). We would like to call out at this point that managing our impulses is not about ignoring or suppressing our emotions—rather it is about understanding our emotional triggers and reactions, and being mindful of how we will respond. If we ignore this, or in any way validate or defend our impulsive behavior, it could have a significant impact on our own performance, the performance of our team, and the relationships we have with others.

Tips for Managing Our Impulses:

- Go to the balcony to gain perspective.
- Check your assumptions about the situation before taking action (review fundamental attribution error from Chapter 3).
- Check in with another person to get their perspective on the event.
- In the moment, take several deep breaths to calm the mind.
- Understand your "hot buttons" and what can trigger them; have a plan for how you will respond when you feel a hot button being pushed (e.g., pinch your wrist, walk away, and so on).

## Optimism

*Perpetual optimism is a force multiplier.*

—*Colin Powell*

People need to know that their leaders believe there is hope in the future. That is not to say there doesn't need to be acknowledgment that there may be challenges to address; in fact this will almost always be the case (under the framework of EI, this is known as *reality testing*). But at the end of the day, folks want to know that things can be better in the future. Therefore, leaders need to be able to assess their own orientation toward optimism.

Fortunately, Martin Seligman has made it easier for us to do this. Often considered the father of the positive psychology movement, Seligman's book, *Learned Optimism*, provides not just a thorough explanation of the differences between optimism and pessimism, but also a self-assessment that helps one determine their own individual "explanatory style" (how we explain events to ourselves) (Seligman 2006). Optimists see bad events as being temporary in nature, only affecting a specific aspect of their lives, and do not overly personalize their role in the event. Pessimists, on the other hand, see negative events as being long-lasting (more permanent), affecting many aspects or areas of their lives (pervasive), and they, in some way, bear personal responsibility (personalization) for the problem or challenge.

These three areas, permanence, pervasiveness, and personalization, are the "3-Ps" Seligman calls out as the primary factors influencing how we explain events to ourselves. Furthermore, these same forces are at play when we experience positive things in our lives. So it is also possible to be optimistic or pessimistic about *good* events. This distinction is one of the key elements that we believe sets Seligman's work apart. In fact, it is possible for a person to be optimistic about bad events, but pessimistic about good events.

The optimism assessment can be found at this website: www.authentichappiness.sas.upenn.edu/testcenter

Questions leaders should ask themselves when assessing their own orientation to optimism:

- When your team encounters challenges, do you communicate a sense of hope that they can address the challenge and succeed, or do you tend to bemoan the fact that things aren't going as planned?
- When you personally experience disappointment, do you believe it will only affect you temporarily, or for a longer period of time?

# Leader as Coach

This chapter has been primarily focused on the leader understanding how their own behaviors and actions impact the team, and what skills, attitudes, and strategies will help leaders manage their own behaviors and make stronger connections with their teams. This section will highlight the role of the leader as coach, and provide tips on specific coaching strategies.

First, it must be understood that coaching is about focusing on the growth and development of another. It is not, in our minds, about the performance evaluation process. Certainly, performance may be impacted as a result of the coaching, and there is clearly a time and place for formal evaluation processes, but the intent here is to focus on the development itself. Therefore, we suggest that, when coaching members of their team, leaders be explicit that the purpose is to focus on the ongoing development of the individual members of the team (or the team itself). In this context, development is about furthering one's skills and competencies, both in technical and in nontechnical situations (e.g., communication skills).

James Flaherty's book, *Coaching: Evoking Excellence in Others*, suggests coaching has three primary functions:

- To achieve long-term, excellent performance
- To gain the ability to self-correct (identify and correct behavior that runs counter to achieving one's goals)
- To engage in generative (ongoing) growth and development (Flaherty 2006)

From this perspective one of the key skills for the leader as coach is to ask really good questions and then to be an even better listener. Asking open-ended, thought-provoking questions results in team members having to engage in a reflective process, taking time to consider their response. Asking questions first also protects the leader from lapsing into solving the problem, lecturing, or defending a position. Coaching invites the leader to focus on the needs of the team member and getting the person to reflect on how they want to further develop themselves and what actions they believe they can take.

Suggested Coaching Actions:

- Set the expectation that you believe ongoing development is important and that it will be an area of focus.
- Ask your team members/direct reports what aspects of themselves they further want to develop, and how you, as the leader, can help support them in that effort.
- Share your own thoughts and ideas about development opportunities and how you believe improving in these areas will make the individual more effective as a team member.
- Work with the individual to identify one to two development goals—but make sure the goals come from the individual and are not the goals *you* want them to pursue (think back to the section on ownership).
- Collaborate with the individual to create a development plan; the plan should include new behaviors to practice, methods for receiving feedback, and a reflection process such as journaling.
- Follow up regularly to check on progress.

## Leader as Educator

Sometimes it makes sense for you, as the leader, to assume the role of educator. For instance, there may be a new clinical or administrative process that the team now needs to use, and you have firsthand knowledge of it. In these situations it would make sense for you to step up and provide the education or training. This is equally true for teaching the skills of self-awareness, interpersonal skills, communication, and so on. In fact, every concept we have surfaced in this book provides an opportunity for leaders to teach these ideas and skills to others.

Act in the role of a facilitator, not a lecturer. Find creative ways to engage your team in conversation about the topic you wish them to learn more about—for example, assign an article to have them read ahead of time and, then at the meeting, break them into small groups to talk about their reactions to the article, what they learned, what they agree or disagree with, and how can your team begin practicing the skill or behavior the article discusses. This is just one example, but tapping into the various LS can also provide many creative ways to engage your team.

## In Summary

Leadership is a difficult endeavor. It's hard work. Not knowing one's own blind spots or how others are perceiving specific behaviors only makes it that much more challenging. Thus, it is imperative that leaders understand how their own mindsets and biases contribute to the team culture, both as it currently exists and as they want to see it in the future. Leading the effort of creating adaptive teams requires energy, optimism, patience, perseverance, and sometimes forgiveness. So while it is certainly hard work, the act of leading can also be incredibly rewarding, especially when the team is functioning as a whole. Next, we will take a closer look at team accountability and the actions leaders can take to drive mutual accountability, where accountability to results and team process are both equally valued.

## End of Chapter Reflective Questions

- Reflect back on situations you have found yourself in when you were frustrated with your team members—how did you respond in the moment? What impact did your response have on the team? To what degree are you aware of (and willing to own) your own contribution to the breakdown?
- What do you do to actively increase/enhance your own level of self-awareness? How do you determine whether the steps you take to be more aware of your own behavior are actually working?

## References

Begley, S., and R. Davidson. 2012. *The Emotional Life of Your Brain: How Its Unique Patterns Affect the Way You Think, Feel, and Live-and How You Can Change Them.* Hachette UK.

Day, D.V. 2001. "Leadership Development: A Review in Context." *The Leadership Quarterly* 11, no. 4, pp. 581–613.

Flaherty, J. 2006. *Coaching: Evoking Excellence in Others*. Routledge.

Goleman, D.P. 1995. *Emotional Intelligence: Why It Can Matter More than IQ for Character, Health and Lifelong Achievement*. New York: Bantam Books.

Gyatsho, T., D. Goleman, and R.J. Richardson. 2003. *Destructive Emotions: How Can We Overcome Them? A Scientific Dialogue with the Dalai Lama*. Bantam Books.

Seligman, M. 2006. *Learned Optimism: How to Change Your Mind and Your Life*. Vintage.

Stein, S.J., and H. Book. 2010. *The EQ Edge: Emotional Intelligence and Your Success*, 25. John Wiley & Sons.

Turner, J.R., and R. Müller. 2005. *The Project Manager's Leadership Style as a Success Factor on Projects: A Literature Review*.

Van Velsor, E., and J.B. Leslie. 1995. "Why Executives Derail: Perspectives Across Time and Cultures." *The Academy of Management Executive* 9, no. 4, pp. 62–72.

# CHAPTER 7

# Creating a Culture of Team Accountability

At the end of the day, each team needs to determine how it will assess its performance and how it will hold itself accountable, not only to results but also to team process. Generally, when we think of accountability we focus immediately on results—quality and safety indicators, patient satisfaction scores, employee engagement surveys, and financial results. All of these measures are under intense scrutiny in today's health care environment.

While we certainly acknowledge the importance of focusing on these key metrics, we believe it is also essential to address accountability within the team itself—to the inner workings of the team, if you will. One way to think about the relationship between results (quantitative measures) and team process is with the following diagram:

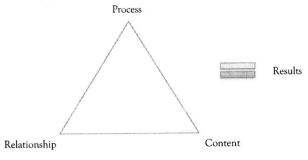

**Figure 7.1 Team process**

In the context of what we want to emphasize, it is really about the team's commitment to each other and to the patients and families (or internal customers) it serves. In Chapter 5 we spent a significant amount of time discussing the concept of ownership and presenting strategies on how to further enhance ownership. When teams are operating from

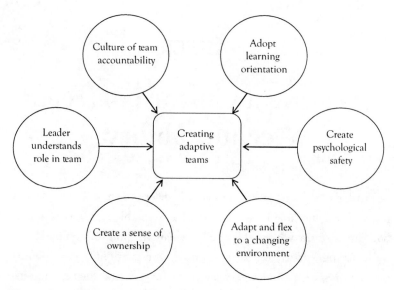

*Figure 7.2  A map for leading adaptive teams*

this position of ownership, everyone feels a responsibility to produce—
produce results, yes, but also to produce for each other.

The framework we have spelled out within the chapters of this book
(see Figure 7.2) can provide a road map for addressing accountability
to the team process. Implementing a learning focus, creating a safe
environment for dialogue, embracing adaptive behaviors, creating ownership, and awareness of how personality, biases, and beliefs impact group
dynamics—all of these areas—can be addressed from the standpoint of
accountability.

Before we dive more deeply into creating accountability processes and
structures in these areas, we will first address, albeit briefly, accountability
to results.

## Accountability to Results

As discussed previously, much has been written and presented on accountability to results in health care, and we are not going to rehash all of
those discussions here; rather we will highlight some of the material that
is available. One of the most notable perspectives on accountability to
results is Kaplan and Norton's work on the balanced scorecard (Norton

and Kaplan 1993). This work was important because it argued that a focus on measurement was just as important in business as it was in science. The notion that if you can't measure it you can't improve it really took flight as a result of that first Harvard Business Review article (along with the work that was occurring in the field of total quality management). The four key areas they called out as ones to systematically measure were: customer results, financial results, internal business processes, and learning and growth (Norton and Kaplan 1993).

Many health care organizations have found it useful to adopt this framework, and consulting groups such as the Studer Group have incorporated this methodology into their own consulting models—the concept of "pillars" used by the Studer Group is one example where organizations create and track measures in the areas of patient satisfaction, quality and safety, employee satisfaction/engagement, and financial performance (Studer 2003).

The benefit of using such an approach is that it helps leaders at all levels pay attention to a variety of metrics, including those that focus on internal processes such as employee engagement and morale. Additionally, since many metrics are now mandated by the federal government, or other regulating agencies (e.g., Hospital Consumer Assessment of Healthcare Providers and Systems (HCAHPS), Leapfrog, etc.), leaders can simply plug these measures into their balanced scorecard categories.

But accountability runs deeper than just tracking performance against these quantitative measures. As addressed at the beginning of this chapter, we really want to focus on accountability to the team and team process.

## Accountability to the Team

One of the problems with using the term *accountability* in our health care organizations is that we all have slightly different perceptions of what the word actually means. Furthermore, this interpretation is based on the social systems we live in and it also implies that our behavior is being monitored (Goodman, Evans, and Carson 2011). In fact, many of the current accountability systems in health care are doing this very thing. It's not that this is necessarily bad; certainly, as consumers of health care we want to ensure that those with whom we entrust our care are following standard protocols and engaging in safe practices. However, there can sometimes be a negative connotation associated with the word. The reason for this is that there is often a perceived accusation that one has not performed adequately. Since (we believe) the vast majority of health care professionals are operating from the best of intentions, and often have a perfectionistic streak, it is not surprising that there can be negative reactions to the word.

*The Oz Principle* explains accountability as "a personal choice to rise above one's circumstances and demonstrate the ownership necessary for achieving desired results" (Connors, Smith, and Hickman 2010). The authors approach accountability from a positive, future-focused perspective by addressing behaviors that lie either "above or below the line." Below-the-line behaviors include finger-pointing, declarations that it is "not my job," and giving up personal responsibility by waiting to be told what to do. Above-the-line behaviors (for which they advocate) are: "see it, own it, solve it." Engaging in these above-the-line behaviors encourages individual ownership of the situation and an unwillingness to pass it off to someone else, or to ignore the situation entirely. We like this approach to both individual and team accountability because it links up nicely with our advocacy for creating a greater sense of ownership within teams.

Considering the diagram we presented earlier, process—content—relationship = results, we would like to focus our attention on process, content, and relationship, and examine it through four of the topic areas we addressed in earlier chapters.

The ability of a team to create a safe environment where all team members feel safe to speak up, share observations, offer feedback, and ask questions is absolutely critical to achieving successful quality and safety outcomes. The health care industry has spent years working on this issue, and yet we still struggle mightily with it. In Chapter 3 we introduced four concepts that leaders can emphasize to create a safer environment for dialogue:

- Suspend assumptions
- Establish a mutual goal
- Practice inquiry
- Empathy

From an accountability standpoint, leaders should make it a habit to routinely conduct an assessment of how the team is performing in these four areas to reinforce the behaviors. A simple way to do this is to dedicate time in one of the standing meetings to conduct the assessment (at the end of a debrief would be one way), in order to assess adherence to the behaviors from two perspectives: (1) how each individual believes they are doing with practicing the behaviors and (2) how the team as a whole is doing. Using a Likert rating scale of 1 to 5 (1 low, 5 high) ask each team member to personally assess how well they are doing in practicing the six behaviors listed previously. Alternatively, the following three open-ended questions can be asked:

- In what ways have you demonstrated these behaviors (and what positive outcomes occurred)?
- In what ways (and in what situations) have you behaved counter to these dialogue skills? What was the impact?
- In what areas, and in what ways, can you continue to further enhance your proficiency with these skills?

It is not necessary that team members share these results with the rest of the group—it can be quite effective to just do the self-reflection. As trust and the comfort level of doing this activity increase, the leader may choose to ask team members to share their results, along with a short explanation of why they answered the way they did.

Likewise, a similar process can be used to assess the team's performance. The use of a Likert scale or asking open-ended questions is an effective way to engage the team in a conversation about how the team is actually doing in practicing these dialogue skills. Using the LS 1-2-4-all can also be a useful way to engage the team in a conversation about how it is doing in using the four dialogue skills.

Another strategy that can be employed is to use Patrick Lencioni's *Five Dysfunctions of a Team* assessment (Lencioni 2002). Lencioni's assessment addresses team functioning through five specific categories:

- Absence of trust
- Fear of conflict

- Lack of commitment
- Avoidance of accountability
- Inattention to results

Asking team members to complete this assessment provides the group with data relative to how they believe they are conducting themselves in these five areas. The team can then decide which areas it needs to focus on and what strategies it will employ to make improvements.

It should also be pointed out that in all of these cases, the leaders need to model the reflective practice and be willing to self-disclose their own answers to the questions posed. This may not be an easy step for all leaders, but it is essential if the goal is to have the team fully engage in the process. For leaders who find it difficult to disclose their own responses, one strategy that can be employed is to first journal about their own responses and identify one to two specific examples they would feel comfortable sharing. This can be a way to ease into sharing the results of the reflective activity. It is not necessary to disclose everything that comes up for the leader—start slow, see how it goes, and build from there.

In Chapter 2 we focused on the strategies for creating a learning environment, and at the end of the chapter we provided some reflective questions for leaders to consider; those questions are also relevant from an accountability standpoint. Since leaders play such a critical role in creating an environment where learning can thrive, they need to pay particular attention to personally assessing what they are doing to create the learning environment, and how it translates to actual performance results (e.g., reviewing the balanced scorecard or pillar goals). Beginning with the five elements listed in the chapter provides a good starting place:

- What has the leader specifically done to foster a learning mindset?
- To what extent is the leader continually exploring how the team can be more flexible and use an adaptive approach?
- How has the leader encouraged positive deviance, and what examples have surfaced as a result?
- To what extent are mistakes being treated as learning opportunities?

- Are debriefs being conducted with regularity, and are the improvement actions identified being acted upon?

In Chapter 4 we identified strategies to help teams become more adaptive, such as assessing and understanding the environment, understanding if they are facing technical or adaptive challenges, and fostering a culture of learning and development.

To this end, leaders can hold themselves and their teams accountable to conducting environmental scans—put it on the calendar for twice a year and make sure you execute. Determining the nature of your challenges (technical or adaptive) is different and requires a different approach. First, it requires gaining knowledge that there is in fact a distinction between technical and adaptive challenges, followed by ongoing education to help people diagnose the nature of these problems. Early on in this effort leaders need to own the responsibility for helping the team with these practices. They need to continually ask the questions of their team and then provide the coaching to help team members with this diagnosis process. The act of being more adaptive fundamentally requires a learning mindset. So this is really about culture change and tracking long-term how behaviors are changing (or not changing).

The idea of accountability to the team provides another lens through which leaders can view accountability. As previously mentioned, accountability to results is certainly important, but so is accountability to team processes and relationships. While there is much focus today on the results side of the equation, we believe there is value in a both/and approach, with an expanded view of accountability, which we also believe benefits long-term performance and strengthens a team's adaptive culture.

## Conclusion

A key belief of ours is that leaders own culture. If, as a health care leader, your intention is to help your team (or teams) become more adaptive so that they are better prepared to respond to a rapidly changing and evolving environment, then this represents a culture change.

The intent of this book is to provide health care leaders with new frameworks and skills that will help their teams excel in this era of complexity and uncertainty. By no means do we believe what is written here captures everything a leader needs to know to be successful. Our hope is simply that leaders are able to relate to the examples that are shared, and are able to put into practice some of the concepts and skills that have been highlighted, with the goal of creating teams that are more adaptive. At the end of the day, we all have the shared goal of improving the health care experience for the patients and families we serve, and to simultaneously ensure our teams are engaged and fulfilled in their work.

# References

Avolio, B.J., and S.T. Hannah. 2008. "Developmental Readiness: Accelerating Leader Development." *Consulting Psychology Journal: Practice and Research* 60, no. 4, p. 331.

Begley, S., and R. Davidson. 2012. *The Emotional Life of Your Brain: How Its Unique Patterns Affect the Way You Think, Feel, and Live-and How You Can Change Them.* Hachette UK.

Belasco, J.A., and R.C. Stayer. 1993. *Flight of the Buffalo.* Dove Audio.

Berwick, D.M. 2003. "Disseminating Innovations in Health Care." *Jama* 289, no. 15, pp. 1969–75.

Connors, R., T. Smith, and C. Hickman. 2010. *The Oz Principle: Getting Results through Individual and Organizational Accountability.* Penguin.

Covey, S.R. 2014. *The 7 Habits of Highly Effective Families.* St. Martin's Press.

Day, D.V. 2001. "Leadership Development:: A Review in Context." *The Leadership Quarterly* 11, no. 4, pp. 581–613.

De Geus, A. 1997. *The Living Company: Habits for Survival in a Turbulent Environment.* London: Nicholas Brealey.

De Geus, A. 2002. *The Living Company: Habits for Survival in a Turbulent Business.* Boston, MA: Harvard Business Review Press.

Decuyper, S., F. Dochy, and P. Van den Bossche. 2010. "Grasping the Dynamic Complexity of Team Learning: An Integrative Model for Effective Team Learning in Organisations." *Educational Research Review* 5, no. 2, pp. 111–33.

Duhigg, C. 2016. "What Google Learned from its Quest to Build the Perfect Team." *The New York Times Magazine,* 26.

Dweck, C.S., and E.L. Leggett. 1988. "A Social-Cognitive Approach to Motivation and Personality." *Psychological Review* 95, no. 2, p. 256.

Edmondson, A.C. 2012. *Teaming: How Organizations Learn, Innovate, and Compete in the Knowledge Economy.* John Wiley & Sons.

Education | Global Partnership for Education. Retrieved from http:// globalpartnership.org/education

Flaherty, J. 2006. *Coaching: Evoking Excellence in Others*. Routledge.

Frankl, V.E. 1985. *Man's Search for Meaning*. Simon and Schuster.

Goleman, D.P. 1995. *Emotional Intelligence: Why It Can Matter More than IQ for Character, Health and Lifelong Achievement*. New York: Bantam Books.

Goodman, J.M., W.R. Evans, and C.M. Carson. 2011. "Organizational Politics and Stress: Perceived Accountability as a Coping Mechanism." *The Journal of Business Inquiry* 10, no. 1, pp. 66–80.

Greenwald, A.G., B.A. Nosek, and M.R. Banaji. 2003. "Understanding and Using the Implicit Association Test: I. An Improved Scoring Algorithm." *Journal of Personality and Social Psychology* 85, no. 2, p. 197.

Greenwald, A.G., M.R. Banaji, L.A. Rudman, S.D. Farnham, B.A. Nosek, and D.S. Mellott. 2002. "A Unified Theory of Implicit Attitudes, Stereotypes, Self-Esteem, and Self-Concept." *Psychological Review* 109, no. 1, p. 3.

Grol, R., and J. Grimshaw. 2003. "From Best Evidence to Best Practice: Effective Implementation of Change in Patients' Care." *The Lancet* 362, no. 9391, pp. 1225–30.

Gyatsho, T., D. Goleman, and R.J. Richardson. 2003. *Destructive Emotions: How Can We Overcome Them?: A Scientific Dialogue with the Dalai Lama*. Bantam Books.

Heath, C., and D. Heath. 2010. *Switch: How to Change When Change is Hard*. New York: Broadway Books.

Heifetz, R., A. Grashow, and M. Linsky. 2009. *The Practice of Adaptive Leadership*. Boston, MA: Harvard Business School Publishing.

Hoffer Gittell, J. 2002. "Coordinating Mechanisms in Care Provider Groups: Relational Coordination as a Mediator and Input Uncertainty as a Moderator of Performance Effects." *Management Science* 48, no. 11, pp. 1408–26.

Kegan, R., and L.L. Lahey. 2009. *Immunity to Change: How to Overcome It and Unlock Potential in Yourself and Your Organization*. Harvard Business Press.

Kegan, R., and L.L. Lahey. 2016. *An Everyone Culture: Becoming a Deliberately Developmental Organization*. Harvard Business Review Press.

King, H.B., J. Battles, D.P. Baker, A. Alonso, E. Salas, J. Webster, L. Toomey, and M. Salisbury. 2008. TeamSTEPPS™: Team Strategies and Tools to Enhance Performance and Patient Safety.

Klein, G., and L. Pierce. 2001. "Adaptive Teams." U.S. Army Research Laboratory sponsored report.

Lencioni, P. 2002. *The Five Dysfunctions of a Team*, 188–89. San Francisco: Iosey-Bass.

Marsh, D.R., D.G. Schroeder, K.A. Dearden, J. Sternin, and M. Sternin. 2004. "The Power of Positive Deviance." *BMJ: British Medical Journal* 329, no. 7475, p. 1177.

Maxfield, D. 2005. *Silence Kills: The Seven Crucial Conversations for Healthcare*. VitalSmarts.

McCandless, K., and H. Lipmanowicz. 2014. *The Surprising Power of Liberating Structures.* Liberating Structures Press.

Norton, D., and R. Kaplan. 1993. "Putting the Balanced Scorecard to Work." *Harvard Business Review* 71, no. 5, pp. 134–40.

Patterson, K. 2002. *Crucial Conversations: Tools for Talking When Stakes are High.* Tata McGraw-Hill Education.

Pink, D.H. 2009. *Drive: The Surprising Truth about What Motivates, 138,* 240. New York, US: Penguin Group, Inc.

Rosenberg, M., and D. Chopra. 2015. *Nonviolent Communication: A Language of Life: Life-Changing Tools for Healthy Relationships.* PuddleDancer Press.

Schein, E.H. 2013. *Humble Inquiry: The Gentle Art of Asking Instead of Telling.* Berrett-Koehler Publishers.

Schwartz, P. 1996. *The Art of the Long View: Paths to Strategic Insight for Yourself and Your Company.* Crown Business.

Seligman, M. 2006. *Learned Optimism: How to Change Your Mind and Your Life.* Vintage.

Senge, P. 1990. *The Fifth Discipline: The Art and Science of the Learning Organization.* New York: Currency Doubleday.

Stein, S.J., and H. Book. 2010. *The EQ Edge: Emotional Intelligence and Your Success, 25.* John Wiley & Sons.

Studer, Q. 2003. *Hardwiring Excellence: Purpose Worthwhile Work Making a Difference.* Fire Starter Pub.

Turner, J.R., and R. Müller. 2005. *The Project Manager's Leadership Style as a Success Factor on Projects: A Literature Review.*

Ury, W. 1991. *Getting Past No: Negotiating in Difficult Situations.* Bantam.

Van Velsor, E., and J.B. Leslie. 1995. "Why Executives Derail: Perspectives Across Time and Cultures." *The Academy of Management Executive* 9, no. 4, pp. 62–72.

Vogt, E.E. 1995. "Learning Out of Context." *Learning Organizations: Developing Cultures for Tomorrow's Workplace,* pp. 293–303.

Weick, K.E., and K.M. Sutcliffe. 2011. *Managing the Unexpected: Resilient Performance in an Age of Uncertainty, 8.* John Wiley & Sons.

Wisdom, J., and H. Wei. 2017. "Cultivating Great Teams: What Health Care Can Learn from Google." Retrieved from http://catalyst.nejm.org/psychological-safety-great-teams

Wong, L. 2004. *Developing Adaptive Leaders: The Crucible Experience of Operation Iraqi Freedom.* Carlisle, PA: Strategic Studies Institute, US Army War College.

Zimmerman, B., P. Reason, L. Rykert, L. Gitterman, J. Christian, and M. Gardam. 2013. "Front-line Ownership: Generating a Cure Mindset for Patient Safety." *Healthc Pap* 13, no. 1, pp. 6–22.

# Index

## OTHER TITLES IN OUR HEALTHCARE MANAGEMENT COLLECTION

David Dilts, Oregon Health & Science University (OHSU)
and Lawrence Fredendall, Clemson University, Editors

- *Quality Management in a Lean Health Care Environment* by Daniel Collins and Melissa Mannon
- *Improving Healthcare Management at the Top: How Balanced Boardrooms Can Lead to Organizational Success* by Milan Frankl and Sharon Roberts
- *The Patient Paradigm Shifts: Profiling the New Healthcare Consumer* by Judy L. Chan

Business Expert Press has over 30 collection in business subjects such as finance, marketing strategy, sustainability, public relations, economics, accounting, corporate communications, and many others. For more information about all our collections, please visit www.businessexpertpress.com/collections.

## Announcing the Business Expert Press Digital Library

*Concise e-books business students need for classroom and research*

This book can also be purchased in an e-book collection by your library as

- a one-time purchase,
- that is owned forever,
- allows for simultaneous readers,
- has no restrictions on printing, and
- can be downloaded as PDFs from within the library community.

Our digital library collections are a great solution to beat the rising cost of textbooks. E-books can be loaded into their course management systems or onto students' e-book readers.
The **Business Expert Press** digital libraries are very affordable, with no obligation to buy in future years. For more information, please visit **www.businessexpertpress.com/librarians**. To set up a trial in the United States, please email **sales@businessexpertpress.com**.

CPSIA information can be obtained
at www.ICGtesting.com
Printed in the USA
FFOW02n0414161217
43960191-43076FF